the creative KITCHEN

LEISURE ARTS, INC.
Little Rock, Arkansas

EDITORIAL STAFF

Editor-in-Chief: Susan White Sullivan
Craft Publications Director: Cheryl Johnson
Special Projects Director: Susan Frantz Wiles
Senior Prepress Director: Mark Hawkins
Art Publications Director: Rhonda Shelby
Technical Editor: Mary Sullivan Hutcheson
Foods Editor: Jane Kenner Prather
Contributing Test Kitchen Assistants: Marcelle Castleberry, Nora Faye Spencer Clift, and Rose Glass Klein
Special Projects Designer: Patricia A. Wallenfang
Designers: Anne Pulliam Stocks and Becky Werle
Lead Graphic Artist: Lora Puls
Graphic Artists: Dayle Carroza, Jacob Casleton, Kara Darling, Becca Snider and Amy Temple
Senior Publications Designer: Dana Vaughn
Imaging Technician: Stephanie Johnson
Prepress Technician: Janie Marie Wright
Photography Manager: Katherine Laughlin
Contributing Photographers: Mark Mathews
Contributing Photo Stylists: Christy Myers
Publishing Systems Administrator: Becky Riddle
Mac Information Technology Specialist: Robert Young

BUSINESS STAFF

President and Chief Executive Officer: Rick Barton
Vice President and Chief Operations Officer: Tom Siebenmorgen
Vice President of Sales: Mike Behar
Director of Finance and Administration: Laticia Mull Dittrich
National Sales Director: Martha Adams
Creative Services: Chaska Lucas
Information Technology Director: Hermine Linz
Controller: Francis Caple
Vice President, Operations: Jim Dittrich
Retail Customer Service Manager: Stan Raynor
Print Production Manager: Fred F. Pruss

Library of Congress Control Number: 2011928279
ISBN-13: 978-1-60900-124-7

the creative KITCHEN

Need an amazing gift? These delicious foods and beverages are wonderful to share—and it's easy to make them look as good as they taste! A savory Garden Chicken Casserole in a place mat Casserole Tote is a perfect way to welcome new neighbors. Why not give your favorite host or hostess a Butterscotch Coffee Cake in a Decorated Cake Box? For someone who likes healthy snacks, put carrots and celery in a Garden Fresh Tote and add a jar of Roasted Olive Dip. Need an elegant gift for a special evening? Place Italian Cream Liqueur in a Bottle Bag that's stapled, not sewn! You'll find ideas to please coffee or tea lovers, ice cream aficionados, and anyone who adores homemade fudge or gourmet popcorn. There are also holiday inspirations, such as cookie-filled treat bags for Halloween and boxed cupcakes for Easter. With more than 100 recipes and quick, creative presentations, you will always have the right gift for the occasion.

table of contents

Guilt-Free Snack Chips

SALSA

ITALIAN CREAM LIQUEUR

Liqueur may be stored in refrigerator up to 1 month.

- 1$\frac{1}{2}$ cups whipping cream
- 1 can (14 ounces) sweetened condensed milk
- 1 bottle (375 ml) hazelnut liqueur
- $\frac{3}{4}$ cup vodka
- 1 teaspoon vanilla extract
- $\frac{1}{2}$ teaspoon almond extract

Place all ingredients in a blender or food processor. Process briefly until completely blended. Pour into bottles and store in refrigerator.

Serve chilled.

Yield: about 2$\frac{3}{4}$ pints liqueur

BOTTLE BAG

Fabric and a stapler are the main "ingredients" you need to construct this no-sew gift bag. Fold a fabric length (one that will go around the bottle a bit more than halfway and is twice the height of the bottle plus 4") in half with the right sides together. Staple the sides together, staying close to fabric edges; turn the bag right side out and pink the top edge. Fold fabric circles (pattern, page 150) in half, arrange in a flower shape, and staple the middle. Place the bottle in the bag, tie with twill tape, and staple on the fabric flowers.

WINE PUNCH

- 2 bottles (750 ml each) dry white wine
- 2 cans (12 ounces each) frozen pineapple juice concentrate, thawed
- ³/₄ cup frozen lemonade concentrate, thawed
- ³/₄ cup frozen orange juice concentrate, thawed
- 1 jar (10 ounces) maraschino cherries

In a 1 gallon container, combine wine, pineapple, lemonade and orange juice concentrates, stirring until well blended. Stir in cherries. Cover and chill 8 hours or overnight to allow flavors to blend. Serve chilled.

Yield: about 3 quarts

SERVE YOURSELF!

A length of chain, a couple of jump rings, and a label holder combine with scrapbook paper and rub-on letters to fashion a clever "necklace" telling what type of beverage is being served. Tie coordinating ribbons around the lid and secure with a colorful button. Catch drips with a laminated scrapbook paper "doily".

GOLDEN BREAKFAST PUNCH

For a casual party, serve in canning jars.

- 2 cups boiling water
- 2 tea bags
- 3 cups orange juice
- 2 cups lemon juice
- 1¹/₂ to 2 cups sugar
- 1 quart dry white wine
- 1 cup vodka
  Garnish: mint leaves

Pour boiling water over tea bags in a heat-resistant container and steep 5 minutes. Remove tea bags. In a gallon container, add tea, juices, and sugar; stir until sugar is dissolved. Cool.

Stir in wine and vodka; chill. Serve over ice. Garnish, if desired.

Yield: about 3 quarts

MINT TEA MIX

1½ cups loose tea leaves
1 jar (0.25 ounces) dried mint leaves
2 tablespoons dried orange peel
2 tablespoons whole cloves

Combine all ingredients in a medium bowl; stir until well blended. Give with serving instructions.
Yield: about 1¾ cups mix

To serve: For 1 cup of tea, add 1 teaspoon tea mix to an individual tea infuser and place in cup. Add boiling water and allow to steep 3 to 5 minutes; remove infuser. Serve hot.

SPICED CRANBERRY TEA MIX

1 cup unsweetened instant tea
1 cup sugar
½ cup orange-flavored instant breakfast drink
2 packages (3 ounces each) cranberry gelatin
1 teaspoon ground cinnamon
1 teaspoon ground allspice

Combine all ingredients until well blended. Give with serving instructions.
Yield: about 2½ cups mix

To serve: Pour 6 ounces hot water over 2 tablespoons tea mix; stir until well blended.

ROYAL-TEA

Give a gift fit for a queen by wrapping a plastic bag full of tea mix in a lady's vintage hankie and then nestling the hankie in a flea-market-find teacup. Add a simple layered tag with the tea name on the front and serving instructions on the back.

Spiced Cranberry
Tea Mix

BAVARIAN MINT CREAMER

- $3/4$ cup non-dairy coffee creamer
- $3/4$ cup confectioners sugar
- $1/2$ cup Dutch process cocoa
- $1/2$ teaspoon peppermint extract

Combine all ingredients in a container with a tight-fitting lid. Shake well to blend. Give with serving instructions.
Yield: about 2 cups creamer

To serve: Stir 2 tablespoons of creamer into 6 ounces of coffee.

AMARETTO CREAMER

- $3/4$ cup non-dairy coffee creamer
- $3/4$ cup confectioners sugar
- 1 teaspoon almond extract
- 1 teaspoon ground cinnamon

Combine all ingredients in a container with a tight-fitting lid. Shake well to blend. Give with serving instructions.
Yield: about $1^1/2$ cups creamer

To serve: Stir 2 tablespoons of creamer into 6 ounces of coffee.

COFFEE LOVER'S DREAM

Fulfill your friend's dream of being a barista by giving her this coffee lover's basket. Place flavored creamers in zip-top plastic bags and add an eye-catching label over the bag top. Look for non-traditional items to use for gift-giving like this aluminum container lined with a graphic dish towel.

LEMON-NUT BREAD

- ³/₄ cup butter or margarine, softened
- 1¹/₂ cups sugar
- 3 eggs
- 2¹/₄ cups all-purpose flour
- ¹/₄ teaspoon salt
- ¹/₄ teaspoon baking soda
- ¹/₄ cup buttermilk
- ³/₄ cup chopped pecans
- Grated zest of 1 lemon
- ³/₄ cup confectioners sugar
- 6 tablespoons freshly squeezed lemon juice

Grease and flour a 5" x 9" loaf pan. In a large bowl, beat butter and sugar until fluffy.

Add eggs; beat until smooth. In a medium bowl, combine flour, salt, and baking soda. Alternately add dry ingredients and buttermilk to butter mixture; stir just until moistened. Stir in pecans and lemon zest. Spoon batter into prepared pan. Bake in a preheated 325° oven for 1¹/₄ hours or until a toothpick inserted in center of loaf comes out clean. Cool in pan 15 minutes.

Remove from pan and place on a wire rack with waxed paper underneath. In a small bowl, combine confectioners sugar and lemon juice. Use a toothpick to punch holes in top of warm bread; pour glaze over bread. Cool bread completely.

Yield: 1 loaf

WELCOMING BREAD

Nothing says "Welcome To the Neighborhood" like freshly baked bread! Bake a loaf (or two) of this delicious Lemon-Nut Bread and give to the new neighbors in a colorful fabric wrapper. Just fold a 34" x 9" piece of fabric in half (match the right sides and short ends) and sew up the sides with a ¹/₂" seam allowance. Turn the wrapper right side out and press the top edge 2" to the inside. Slip a wrapped loaf inside and tie closed with a colorful ribbon. Tie on a coordinating punched cardstock label.

Lemon-Nut
Bread

MUFFIN BASKET LINER

Welcome the new neighbors with tasty muffins in a lined basket. Hem a fabric piece that fits the basket; use clear nylon thread to sew jumbo rickrack to the liner edges. Use pinking shears to cut the flower and leaf pieces (patterns, page 151) from scrap fabrics and felt. Layer the flower pieces and gather at the center. Sew the flower, leaves, and a fabric-covered button to the liner.

CHERRY-BERRY MUFFINS

- 2 cups all-purpose flour
- 1 cup quick-cooking oats
- 1/3 cup firmly packed brown sugar
- 1/3 cup granulated sugar
- 3/4 teaspoon baking soda
- 3/4 teaspoon baking powder
- 1/4 teaspoon salt
- 3/4 cup buttermilk
- 1/2 cup butter or margarine, melted
- 2 eggs
- 1 teaspoon vanilla extract
- 1 package (11 ounces) white chocolate baking chips
- 1 cup coarsely chopped maraschino cherries
- 1 cup fresh blueberries

Line muffin pans with paper baking cups; set aside.

In a large bowl, combine flour, oats, sugars, baking soda, baking powder, and salt. In a small bowl, combine buttermilk, melted butter, eggs, and vanilla. Make a well in center of dry ingredients and add buttermilk mixture to dry ingredients; stir just until moistened. Stir in white chocolate chips, cherries, and blueberries. Spoon batter into prepared pans, filling each cup about 2/3 full.

Bake in a preheated 375° oven for 18 to 22 minutes or until lightly browned and a toothpick inserted in center of muffin comes out clean. Serve warm or cool on a wire rack.
Yield: about 2 dozen

PUMPKIN-CHOCOLATE CHIP MUFFINS

- 1 cup canned pumpkin
- 1 cup firmly packed brown sugar
- 2 eggs
- 1/4 cup vegetable oil
- 3 cups all-purpose baking mix
- 1 teaspoon pumpkin pie spice
- 1 cup semisweet chocolate chips
- 3/4 cup chopped pecans, toasted

Line muffin pans with paper baking cups; set aside.

In a large bowl, combine pumpkin, brown sugar, eggs, and oil. Add baking mix and pumpkin pie spice; beat just until blended. Stir in chocolate chips and pecans. Spoon batter into prepared pans, filling each cup about 2/3 full.

Bake in a preheated 400° oven for 14 to 18 minutes or until golden brown and a toothpick inserted in center of muffin comes out clean. Serve warm or cool on a wire rack.
Yield: about 1 1/2 dozen

DILL & GREEN ONION BREAD

- 1 package dry yeast
- 1 cup warm milk (105°-115°)
- 1/4 cup butter or margarine, softened
- 1/4 cup sugar
- 1 egg
- 2 tablespoons finely chopped fresh dill weed
- 2 tablespoons finely chopped green onions
- 1 teaspoon salt
- 3³/₄ to 4 cups all-purpose flour
  Vegetable oil cooking spray
- 1 egg
- 1 tablespoon water
  Fresh dill sprigs and pieces of green onion blades to decorate

In a small bowl, dissolve yeast in warm milk. In a large bowl, combine butter, sugar, 1 egg, chopped dill weed, chopped onions, salt, and yeast mixture; beat until blended. Add 3³/₄ cups flour; stir until a soft dough forms. Turn onto a lightly floured surface and knead about 5 minutes or until dough becomes smooth and elastic, adding additional flour as necessary. Place in a large bowl sprayed with cooking spray, turning once to coat top of dough. Cover and let rise in a warm place (80° to 85°) 1 hour or until doubled in size.

Turn dough onto a lightly floured surface and punch down. Divide dough into fourths.

Shape into two 4¹/₂" round loaves and two 12" long baguette loaves. Place on 2 greased baking sheets. Spray tops of dough with cooking spray, cover, and let rise in a warm place 1 hour or until doubled in size.

In a small bowl, beat remaining egg and water; brush over loaves. Decorate with dill sprigs and green onion blades. Brush decorations with egg mixture.

Bake in a preheated 350° oven for 20 to 25 minutes or until bread is golden brown and sounds hollow when tapped. Serve warm or transfer to a wire rack to cool.

Yield: 4 loaves

BREAD WRAP

Use matching colors of embroidery floss to work *Running Stitches* (page 145) along the stripes of a cotton dish towel. Wrap a freshly baked loaf in the towel and tie with floss. Include the bread recipe with a coordinating card.

PRALINE BISCUITS

- 1 cup chopped pecans
- 1/4 cup firmly packed brown sugar
- 3 tablespoons butter or margarine, melted
- 1 teaspoon maple extract
- 2 cups all-purpose flour
- 2 teaspoons granulated sugar
- 1 teaspoon baking powder
- 1/2 teaspoon baking soda
- 1/4 teaspoon salt
- 1/2 cup vegetable shortening
- 3/4 cup milk

In a small bowl, combine pecans, brown sugar, butter, and maple extract; set aside.

In a medium bowl, combine flour, granulated sugar, baking powder, baking soda, and salt. Using a pastry blender or 2 knives, cut shortening into dry ingredients until mixture resembles coarse meal. Add milk, stirring just until moistened.

Turn dough onto a lightly floured surface and knead about 2 minutes. Roll out dough into an 8" x 12" rectangle; spread pecan mixture over dough. Beginning at 1 long edge, roll up dough jellyroll style. Using a serrated knife, cut into twelve 1" thick slices. Place slices with sides touching in a greased 7" x 11" baking pan.

Bake in a preheated 400° oven for 22 to 25 minutes or until lightly browned. Remove from pan and serve warm.
Yield: 1 dozen

APPLIQUÉD TEA TOWEL

Wake up someone's morning with this "tweet" appliquéd tea towel! Fusible web appliqués (patterns, page 152) and simple embroidery stitches (page 144), along with buttons and rickrack, create a cheery basket liner for these delicious biscuits.

the creative KITCHEN 21

CHERRY MUFFINS

　　1　jar (10 ounces) maraschino cherries
1³/₄　cups all-purpose flour
　¹/₂　cup sugar
2¹/₂　teaspoons baking powder
　　1　teaspoon dried lemon peel
　³/₄　teaspoon salt
　¹/₂　cup milk
　¹/₃　cup vegetable oil
　　1　egg
　　1　teaspoon almond extract
　¹/₄　cup chopped slivered almonds

Line muffin pan with paper baking cups; set aside.

Reserving ¹/₄ cup cherry juice, drain and coarsely chop cherries. In a small bowl, whisk reserved cherry juice, milk, oil, egg, and almond extract. In a large bowl, stir together flour, sugar, baking powder, lemon peel, and salt. Make a well in center of dry ingredients and add egg mixture; stir just until moistened. Stir in cherries and almonds. Spoon batter into prepared pan, filling each cup ³/₄ full.

Bake in a preheated 400° oven for 18 to 20 minutes or until edges are lightly browned. Remove from pan; serve warm or cool on a wire rack.

Yield: about 1 dozen

ALMOND MUFFINS

1¹/₃　cups all-purpose flour
　¹/₂　cup firmly packed brown sugar
　　1　teaspoon baking powder
　¹/₂　teaspoon baking soda
　¹/₄　teaspoon salt
　　1　cup plus 2 tablespoons chopped sliced almonds, toasted and divided
　¹/₂　cup buttermilk
　¹/₄　cup butter or margarine, melted
　　2　eggs, beaten
　¹/₂　teaspoon vanilla extract
　¹/₂　teaspoon almond extract

Line muffin pan with paper baking cups; set aside.

In a medium bowl, combine flour, brown sugar, baking powder, baking soda, and salt. Stir in 1 cup almonds. In a small bowl, combine buttermilk, melted butter, eggs, and extracts. Make a well in center of dry ingredients and add buttermilk mixture; stir just until moistened. Spoon batter into prepared pan, filling each cup about ¹/₂ full. Sprinkle remaining 2 tablespoons almonds over batter.

Bake in a preheated 350° oven for 15 to 18 minutes or until lightly browned and a toothpick inserted in center of muffin comes out clean. Remove from pan; serve warm or cool on a wire rack.

Yield: about 1 dozen

FRIENDSHIP MUFFINS

Cute crocheted cherries (found at the local scrapbook store) hint at the rich flavor of the muffins. The layered scrapbook paper tag gets a pretty finish from glitter and a heartfelt stamped message.

ORANGE-OATMEAL ROLLS

- 1 package (16 ounces) hot roll mix
- 1 cup sweetened crunchy oat cereal
- 1 cup very warm orange juice (120° to 130°)
- 2 tablespoons honey
- 2 tablespoons butter or margarine, melted
- 1 egg
- 1 tablespoon grated orange zest
- $^1/_2$ cup coarsely ground pecans Vegetable cooking spray
- 1 cup confectioners sugar
- 5 teaspoons orange juice

Combine hot roll mix and yeast from roll mix with cereal. Stir in 1 cup very warm orange juice, honey, melted butter, egg, and orange zest; stir until well blended. Stir in pecans. Turn onto a lightly floured surface and knead 3 minutes or until dough becomes smooth and elastic. Cover dough; allow to rest 10 minutes.

Shape dough into eighteen balls. Place in a greased 9" x 12" aluminum foil baking pan. Spray top of dough with cooking spray, cover, and let rise in a warm place (80° to 85°) for 1 hour or until almost doubled in size.

Bake in a preheated 375° oven for 15 to 20 minutes or until golden brown. Cool in pan.

Combine confectioners sugar and 5 teaspoons orange juice in a small bowl; stir until smooth. Drizzle icing over rolls. Allow icing to harden.
Yield: 18 rolls

A WELCOMED GIFT

A simple pan of Orange-Oatmeal Rolls is dressed up for gift-giving with a unique card. Cut a paper band that will go around the pan. Cut a card holder (pattern, page 153) from cardstock and attach to the band with brads. Layer and glue a ribbon-loop flower, a paper circle, and a vintage button on the card holder. Secure the paper band around the rolls. Print a special message or the recipe on a 3" x 6$^1/_2$" piece of scrapbook paper. Layer the paper on cardstock and glue a stamped and layered circle to the card top. To make the card pocket, cut 2 pieces of brown paper about $^3/_4$" larger than the card; cut a notch from the front piece at the top. Stitch the paper pieces together along the side and bottom edges. Place the card in the pocket and slide the pocket under the card holder.

ORANGE SPICE BREAD

    2 packages (7 ounces each) bran muffin mix
$^1/_2$ cup raisins
    2 eggs
$^1/_2$ cup orange juice concentrate, thawed
$^1/_2$ cup orange marmalade, divided
$^1/_4$ cup vegetable oil
$^1/_4$ cup milk
    2 teaspoons ground allspice

In a medium bowl, combine muffin mix and raisins. Add eggs, orange juice concentrate, 6 tablespoons orange marmalade, oil, milk, and allspice; stir until well-blended. Pour into 4 greased and floured $5^3/_4$" x $3^1/_4$" loaf pans. Bake in a preheated 400° oven for 20 to 25 minutes or until a toothpick inserted in center comes out clean.

Remove loaves from pans and place on a wire rack. Spread remaining 2 tablespoons orange marmalade evenly over tops of hot loaves.
Yield: 4 mini loaves

PINEAPPLE-PUMPKIN BREAD

  1 package (16 ounces) pound cake mix
  2 teaspoons pumpkin pie spice
  1 teaspoon baking soda
  1 cup canned pumpkin
  1 can (8 ounces) crushed pineapple, undrained
  2 eggs
  1 cup chopped pecans

Line bottoms of two $8^1/_2$" x $4^1/_2$" loaf pans with waxed paper. Grease and flour waxed paper and sides of pans; set aside.

In a large bowl, combine first 3 ingredients. Add pumpkin, pineapple, and eggs; beat until well blended. Stir in pecans. Spoon batter into prepared pans. Bake in a preheated 325° oven for 45 to 55 minutes or until a toothpick inserted in center of bread comes out clean. Remove from pans after 20 minutes.
Yield: 2 loaves

SWEET DESSERT BREADS
Wrap a yummy dessert bread with plastic wrap and then add fun scrapbook paper and vellum bands held in place with lively ribbons. Write your message on a coordinating tag, slip into a vellum envelope, and you've a sweet treat that can't be beat.

pineapple - pumpkin bread

APRICOT-ALMOND ROLLS
YEAST DOUGH
- 1 package quick-acting dry yeast
- 1/4 cup plus 1 teaspoon sugar, divided
- 1/4 cup warm water
- 1 3/4 cups milk
- 1/3 cup butter or margarine
- 1 teaspoon salt
- 5 to 6 cups all-purpose flour, divided
- 1 egg
- Vegetable cooking spray

APRICOT-ALMOND FILLING
- 1 1/2 cups apricot preserves
- 3/4 cup sugar
- 1 1/2 cups sliced almonds

ALMOND GLAZE
- 1 1/2 cups confectioners sugar
- 2 tablespoons water
- 1 teaspoon almond extract

In a small bowl, dissolve yeast and 1 teaspoon sugar in 1/4 cup warm water. In a small saucepan, heat milk, butter, remaining 1/4 cup sugar, and salt over medium heat until butter melts; remove from heat.

In a large bowl, combine 2 cups flour and milk mixture. Beat in yeast mixture and egg; beat until well blended. Add 3 cups flour, 1 cup at a time; stir until a soft dough forms. Turn onto a lightly floured surface. Knead about 5 minutes or until dough becomes smooth and elastic, using additional flour as necessary. Place in a large bowl sprayed with cooking spray, turning once to coat top of dough. Cover and let rise in a warm place (80° to 85°) 1 1/4 hours or until doubled in size.

Turn dough onto a lightly floured surface and punch down. Divide dough into thirds. Roll each third into a 10" x 14" rectangle.

For filling, combine apricot preserves and sugar in a small bowl; stir until well blended. Spread 1/3 of apricot mixture on each dough piece. Evenly sprinkle with almonds.

Beginning at 1 short edge, roll up each rectangle jellyroll style. Pinch seams to seal. Cut dough into ten 1" slices. Place each roll, cut side down, in a greased 8" round baking pan. Spray rolls with cooking spray, cover, and let rise in a warm place about 40 minutes or until doubled in size.

Bake in a preheated 350° oven for 20 to 27 minutes or until golden brown. Cool in pans 10 minutes.

For glaze, combine confectioners sugar, water, and almond extract in a small bowl; stir until smooth. Drizzle glaze over warm rolls. Serve warm or cool completely.
Yield: 3 pans, 10 rolls each

PICTURE PERFECT BIRTHDAY

Send birthday greetings with these delicious sweet rolls. Decorate the plastic lid with a scrapbook paper round; wrap colorful ribbon around the pan and clip to the sides with mini clothespins. Wrap a small frame in ribbon and fabric; then embellish with crocheted leaves and a flower (available with scrapbooking supplies), a leaf charm, a dimensional sticker, a button, and velvet ribbon. Use removable tape to attach the frame to the lid.

EASY ALMOND-CINNAMON ROLLS

- 1/2 cup firmly packed brown sugar, divided
- 1/2 cup butter or margarine, melted and divided
- 4 tablespoons amaretto, divided
- 1/2 teaspoon ground cinnamon, divided
- 2/3 cup sliced almonds, divided
- 1 package (25 ounces) frozen white dinner rolls, divided

Combine 1/4 cup brown sugar, 1/4 cup melted butter, 2 tablespoons amaretto, and 1/4 teaspoon cinnamon in an 8 1/2" round baking pan. Stir in 1/3 cup almonds. Place half of frozen dinner rolls on top of almond mixture. Repeat with second pan and remaining ingredients. Cover and place in refrigerator overnight. Give with serving instructions.
Yield: 2 pans, about 12 rolls each

To serve: Remove pan of rolls from refrigerator. Loosely cover rolls and let rise in a warm place (80° to 85°) 1 to 2 hours or until doubled in size.

Bake, uncovered, in lower half of a preheated 350° oven for 15 to 18 minutes or until rolls are lightly browned. Cool in pan 5 minutes. Invert rolls onto a serving dish. Serve immediately.

FRESH-AS-SPRING TOTE

Give your best quilting buddy a batch of fresh and tasty rolls in a fabric collage bag that goes together in no time. Arrange several coordinating fabrics on the web side of paper-backed fusible web. Cover the fabrics and web with a piece of aluminum foil and fuse the fabrics to the web. Peel away the foil and excess web and discard. Topstitch and zigzag stitch the fabric collage as desired. Remove the paper backing and fuse the collage to a canvas tote bag. Sew on a few buttons, slip in a pan of the rolls, and head out the door to quilt with your friend.

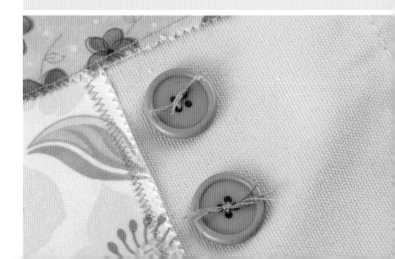

Ultimate Candies

HONEY-NUT FUDGE

- ¼ cup butter or margarine
- 3 ounces unsweetened baking chocolate
- ½ cup honey
- 1 tablespoon water
- 1 teaspoon vanilla extract
- 1 package (16 ounces) confectioners sugar
- 1 cup chopped pecans

Line an 8" square baking pan with aluminum foil, extending foil over 2 sides of pan; grease foil and set aside.

In a heavy large saucepan, melt butter and chocolate over medium-low heat. Add honey, water, and vanilla; stir until well blended. Remove from heat. Add confectioners sugar; stir until smooth. Stir in pecans. Spread mixture into prepared pan. Chill until firm.

Use ends of foil to lift fudge from pan. Cut into 1" squares. Store in a cool place.

Yield: about 4 dozen

CHOCOLATE-PEANUT BUTTER PUFFS

- 1 cup semisweet chocolate chips
- 1 cup peanut butter chips
- ½ cup coarsely chopped peanuts
- 30 marshmallows

In a medium microwave-safe bowl, combine chocolate and peanut butter chips. Microwave on MEDIUM-HIGH (80%) 2 minutes or until mixture softens; stir until smooth. Stir in peanuts. Drop about 4 marshmallows at a time into chocolate mixture; stir to completely cover marshmallows. Place coated marshmallows on a waxed paper-lined baking sheet. Chill until chocolate hardens.

Yield: 2½ dozen

TREATS TO GO

No, it's not Chinese take-out, but those clever boxes can be found in the party section of the craft store. And they're not plain white! Add a monogram sticker and a few buttons to a cardstock tag and glue to the box front. What a cute way to give your favorite candies!

CREAMY LEMON-PECAN CANDIES

1³/₄   cups sugar
  1   cup whipping cream
  1   cup miniature marshmallows
  1   teaspoon dried lemon peel
¹/₂   teaspoon lemon extract
1³/₄   cups chopped pecans

In a large microwave-safe bowl, combine sugar and whipping cream. Microwave on HIGH 8 to 12 minutes or until mixture reaches soft-ball stage on a candy thermometer (approximately 234° to 240°). Test about ¹/₂ teaspoon of mixture in ice water. Mixture will easily form a ball in ice water but will flatten when held in your hand.

Without scraping sides, pour candy into another large heat-resistant bowl. Add marshmallows, lemon peel, and lemon extract; beat 3 to 5 minutes or until mixture thickens and begins to lose its gloss. Stir in pecans. Quickly drop teaspoonfuls of candy onto greased waxed paper; cool completely.
Yield: about 3¹/₂ dozen

PEANUT BUTTER BARS

  1   package (16 ounces) confectioners sugar
1¹/₂   cups graham cracker crumbs
  1   cup smooth peanut butter
  1   cup butter or margarine
  8   chocolate-covered caramel, peanut, and nougat candy bars (2.07 ounces each), chopped
  1   tablespoon milk

Combine confectioners sugar and graham cracker crumbs in a large bowl. In a medium microwave-safe bowl, combine peanut butter and butter. Microwave on MEDIUM-HIGH (80%) 2 minutes or until mixture melts, stirring after each minute. Pour peanut butter mixture over graham cracker mixture; stir until well blended. Press mixture into bottom of an ungreased 9" x 13" baking dish.

Place candy bar pieces and milk in a medium microwave-safe bowl. Microwave on MEDIUM (50%) 3 minutes or until candy melts, stirring after each minute. Spread melted candy mixture over peanut butter mixture. Cool 20 minutes or until candy mixture hardens. Cut into 1" squares.
Yield: about 8 dozen

CANDY BOXES

Send your guests home with sweet homemade confections. Wrap a pretty paper band around a candy box, tie it up with ribbon and a button, and add a stamped or rub-on monogram to a vellum tag.

CREAMY MINT FUDGE

    2 packages (6 ounces each) white
       baking chocolate, chopped
  1/2 cup sweetened condensed milk
 1 1/2 teaspoons vanilla extract
    1 teaspoon mint extract
   10 to 15 drops green food coloring
    1 cup confectioners sugar
  1/2 cup semisweet chocolate chips

Combine white chocolate and sweetened condensed milk in a medium saucepan. Stirring constantly, cook over low heat until chocolate softens. Remove from heat; stir until chocolate melts. Stir in extracts, food coloring, and confectioners sugar. Spread into a greased 8" square baking pan. Chill 30 minutes or until firm.

Place chocolate chips in a small microwave-safe bowl. Microwave on HIGH 1 minute or until chocolate softens; stir until smooth. Spread over fudge. Chill 15 minutes or until chocolate hardens.

Cut into squares. Store in refrigerator.
Yield: about 3 1/2 dozen

MICROWAVE RASPBERRY-PECAN FUDGE

  1/2 cup butter or margarine
 1 1/2 cups sugar
    1 can (5 ounces) evaporated milk
    2 cups miniature marshmallows
    1 cup semisweet chocolate chips
  3/4 cup chopped pecans
    2 tablespoons raspberry-flavored
       liqueur

Line an 8" square baking pan with aluminum foil, extending foil over 2 sides of pan; grease foil. Set pan aside.

In a large microwave-safe bowl, microwave butter on HIGH 1 minute. Stir in sugar and evaporated milk. Microwave on HIGH 8 minutes, stirring every 2 minutes. Stir in marshmallows and chocolate chips. Microwave on MEDIUM-HIGH (80%) 1 minute; stir until mixture is smooth. Stir in pecans and liqueur. Pour mixture into prepared pan; chill.

Use ends of foil to lift fudge from pan. Cut into squares. Store in refrigerator.
Yield: about 3 1/2 dozen

DECORATED FUDGE TIN

A layered felt and fabric flower (patterns, page 149) with a covered button center makes an excellent topper for a candy tin. Stamp the recipe name on a layered cardstock leaf tag that's been cut with pinking shears.

CHOCOLATE CHERRY-ALMOND CREAMS

   1/2 cup butter or margarine, softened
   1   can (14 ounces) sweetened
        condensed milk
   1   teaspoon vanilla extract
   1/2 teaspoon almond extract
   11   cups confectioners sugar
   2   cups slivered almonds, toasted and
        finely chopped
   1   jar (10 ounces) maraschino cherries,
        drained, chopped, and patted dry
   24   ounces chocolate candy coating,
        chopped
   1   package (12 ounces) semisweet
        chocolate chips

In a large bowl, beat butter until fluffy. Add sweetened condensed milk and extracts; beat until well blended. Gradually stir in confectioners sugar, kneading in last 4 cups. Knead in almonds and cherries. Shape mixture into 1" balls. Place on a baking sheet lined with waxed paper. Chill 2 hours or until firm.

In top of a double boiler, melt candy coating and chocolate chips over hot, not simmering, water. Placing each ball on a fork and holding over saucepan, spoon chocolate over balls. Place balls on baking sheet lined with waxed paper. Drizzle remaining chocolate over each candy to decorate. Chill candies about 10 minutes or until chocolate hardens. **Yield:** about 9 dozen

CHOCOLATE DELIGHTS
For the perfect end to a special dinner, give your friends pretty boxes of chocolate treats. Wrap the candy box with a wrapping paper band, tie with a sparkly ribbon, and top with a glittered tag. The ribbon rose (page 148) is actually a pin—what a great accessory!

Cookies for Everyone

CRUNCHY PECAN COOKIES

1	cup butter or margarine, softened
1	cup granulated sugar
1	cup firmly packed brown sugar
1	cup vegetable oil
1	egg
1	teaspoon vanilla extract
3½	cups all-purpose flour
1	teaspoon baking soda
½	teaspoon salt
2	cups finely crushed corn flake cereal
1½	cups chopped pecans

In a large bowl, beat butter and sugars until fluffy. Beat in oil, egg, and vanilla. In a medium bowl, combine flour, baking soda, and salt. Add dry ingredients to butter mixture; stir until a soft dough forms. Stir in cereal crumbs and pecans. Drop tablespoonfuls of dough 2" apart onto a greased baking sheet. Using a fork dipped in water, make a crisscross design on each cookie. Bake in a preheated 350° oven for 10 to 12 minutes or until edges are lightly browned. Cool on wire racks.
Yield: about 7 dozen

COOKIE CANISTERS
Crunchy pecan cookies are kept safe for delivery in these "upcycled" chip and drink mix containers. Jazz up the containers with bright scrapbook paper and a tag tied on with string.

SWEET THANK YOU COOKIE STACKS

Stack several cookies in a paper baking cup and wrap with cellophane; tie closed with pretty ribbons. Personalize a "Thank You!" tag with coordinating scrapbook papers, stickers, and more ribbon. Be sure to share the spicy cookie recipe!

SPICED FRUIT RAVIOLI COOKIES

COOKIES

- ½ cup butter or margarine, softened
- ½ cup granulated sugar
- 1 egg
- 1 tablespoon orange juice
- 1 teaspoon grated orange zest
- 1 teaspoon vanilla extract
- 1½ cups all-purpose flour
- ¼ cup confectioners sugar
- 2 tablespoons cornstarch

FILLING

- ⅔ cup coarsely chopped dried peaches
- ⅓ cup sugar
- ¼ cup water
- 1 tablespoon peach brandy
- ¼ teaspoon ground allspice

For cookies, cream butter and granulated sugar in a large bowl until fluffy. Add egg, orange juice, orange zest, and vanilla; beat until smooth. In a small bowl, combine flour, confectioners sugar, and cornstarch. Add dry ingredients to creamed mixture; stir until a soft dough forms. Divide dough into 4 balls. Wrap in plastic wrap and chill 2 hours or until firm enough to handle.

For filling, combine peaches, sugar, and water in a heavy small saucepan over high heat. Stirring frequently, bring to a boil. Reduce heat to low and cover. Stirring occasionally, simmer 10 to 12 minutes or until most of liquid is absorbed. Stir in peach brandy and allspice. Place peach mixture in a food processor. Pulse process until coarsely puréed; set aside.

Roll 1 ball of dough between sheets of plastic wrap into a 9" circle. Remove top sheet of plastic wrap. Using a 2" round ravioli cutter, lightly mark circles on dough. Place ½ teaspoon of peach mixture in center of each circle. Roll out a second ball of dough between sheets of plastic wrap. Remove top sheet of plastic wrap and invert dough on top of peach-topped dough, matching edges. (There should be 2 layers of dough between 2 sheets of plastic wrap.) Transfer plastic-covered dough onto a baking sheet; chill 20 minutes.

Remove top sheet of plastic wrap. Using ravioli cutter and keeping filling in center of cutter, cut out cookies. Use a spatula to carefully transfer cookies to a greased baking sheet.

Bake in a preheated 350° oven for 8 to 10 minutes or until edges are lightly browned. Transfer cookies to a wire rack to cool. Repeat with remaining dough and filling.
Yield: about 3 dozen

ICE-CREAM CONE COOKIES

COOKIES

- 1 can (8 ounces) almond paste, coarsely crumbled
- $3/4$ cup butter or margarine, softened
- $1/2$ cup granulated sugar
- $1/2$ cup confectioners sugar
- 1 egg
- $1/2$ teaspoon vanilla extract
- $1/8$ teaspoon bubble gum-flavored oil (used in candy making)
- $2 1/4$ cups all-purpose flour

ICING

- 2 cups confectioners sugar
- 3 tablespoons milk
- 10 drops bubble gum-flavored oil (used in candy making)
- Pink paste food coloring
- Pastel confetti sprinkles to decorate

For cookies, place almond paste in a large microwave-safe bowl. Microwave on HIGH 25 seconds to soften. Add butter and sugars to almond paste; beat until fluffy. Add egg, vanilla, and flavored oil; beat until smooth. Gradually add flour; stir until a soft dough forms. Divide dough into thirds. Wrap in plastic wrap and chill 1 hour.

On a lightly floured surface, roll out $1/3$ of dough at a time to $1/4$" thickness. Use a $2 1/2$" x $3 3/4$" ice-cream cone-shaped cookie cutter to cut out cookies. Transfer to a lightly greased baking sheet. Bake in a preheated 350° oven for 7 to 9 minutes or until bottoms are lightly browned. Transfer cookies to a wire rack with waxed paper underneath to cool.

For icing, combine confectioners sugar, milk, and flavored oil in a medium bowl; stir until smooth. Tint pink. Ice tops of cookies to resemble ice cream. Decorate icing with sprinkles before icing hardens. Allow icing to harden.

Yield: about 4 dozen

CLOWNIN' AROUND

Kids will love taking home these fun "ice cream cone" cookies. To package each cookie, draw around the cookie cutter on felt for the clown's head. Add a felt hat, pom-pom hat topper and nose, and a gathered ribbon collar. Simple embroidery stitches (page 144) give the face the details—*French Knots* for hair, *Cross Stitches* for eyes, and a *Backstitch* mouth (color around the stitches with a marker). Place the cookie in a baggie and fold coordinating felt pieces over the top of the bag. Bright brads hold the felt toppers in place; now just glue the clown on top!

BOBBER BOX

Take a round papier-maché box and paint it half white, half red to look like a fishing bobber. Glue a red cardstock square to the lid and punch a hole at the top. A bent paper clip becomes a hook for the "Hooked on You" tag. Fill the box with Fishing Lure Cookies.

FISHING LURE COOKIES

- 1 cup butter or margarine, softened
- 1/3 cup butter-flavored shortening
- 1/3 cup vegetable oil
- 2 cups sugar
- 2 eggs
- 1 teaspoon vanilla extract
- 1 cup blackberry jam
- 6 1/2 cups all-purpose flour
- 1/2 teaspoon salt
- 3 cups water
  Red, green, yellow, purple, orange, blue, and black paste food coloring

In a large bowl, cream butter, shortening, oil, and sugar until fluffy. Add eggs and vanilla; beat until smooth. Stir in jam. In another large bowl, combine flour and salt. Add dry ingredients to creamed mixture; knead until a soft dough forms.

Use a permanent marker to trace fish pattern (below) onto a piece of stencil plastic; cut out. On a lightly floured surface, roll out dough to 1/4" thickness. Place pattern on dough and use a sharp knife to cut out cookies. Transfer to a greased baking sheet. Bake in a preheated 350° oven for 8 to 10 minutes or until lightly browned. Transfer to a wire rack to cool completely.

Pour 1/2 cup water in each of 6 small bowls. Add a small amount of red food coloring to 1 bowl; stir until dissolved. Repeat for all colors except black. To decorate cookies, use a small round paintbrush to lightly brush diluted food coloring onto cookies to resemble fishing lures. Use a small round paintbrush and undiluted food coloring to paint eyes and scales on cookies. Allow to dry. **Yield:** about 6 dozen

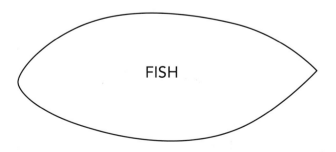

FISH

STRAWBERRY CHEESECAKE BARS

- 1 package (18.25 ounces) strawberry cake mix
- 1 cup chopped pecans, toasted
- ³/₄ cup butter or margarine, melted
- 2 packages (8 ounces each) cream cheese, softened
- 1 cup sugar
- ¹/₃ cup strawberry jam

In a medium bowl, combine cake mix and pecans. Drizzle melted butter over mixture; stir until well blended. Press mixture into bottom of a greased 9" x 13" baking pan. In a medium bowl, beat cream cheese and sugar until smooth. Spread cream cheese mixture over crust.

Process jam in a food processor until smooth. Spoon into a resealable plastic bag. Snip off 1 corner of bag. Pipe lengthwise lines of jam about 1" apart. Use a knife to pull jam from side to side through cream cheese mixture at 1" intervals. Bake in a preheated 350° oven for 18 to 23 minutes or until edges begin to brown and center is set. Cool in pan on a wire rack. Cover and chill 2 hours or until firm.

Cut into 1" x 2" bars. Store in refrigerator.
Yield: about 4 dozen

LOVELY & DELICIOUS
For an elegant presentation of these lovely bars, create a unique cake stand from a vintage plate and pretty saucer-style champagne glass. Invert the glass and use an epoxy adhesive to glue the plate to the glass bottom. Bits of lace, scraps of floral paper, delicate ribbons, cardstock, and a button combine to make a charming gift tag.

CHOCOLATE-HAZELNUT SANDWICH COOKIES

    1   cup butter (not margarine), softened
    1   cup sugar
    1   egg
$1^1/_2$ teaspoons vanilla extract
$1^1/_4$ cups all-purpose flour
    1   cup potato starch flour (also called potato starch, but do not use potato flour)
  $^1/_2$ cup chocolate-hazelnut spread
  $^1/_3$ cup semisweet chocolate chips

Line baking sheets with parchment paper; set aside.

In a large bowl, beat butter and sugar until fluffy. Beat in egg and vanilla. In a medium bowl, combine flour and potato starch flour; add to butter mixture. Stir until a soft dough forms. Chill dough about 2 hours.

Using floured hands, roll dough into 1" balls and place on prepared baking sheets. Slightly flatten balls. Bake in a preheated 375° oven for 8 to 10 or until edges are lightly browned. Place on a wire rack to cool.

Place half of cookies, bottom side up, on waxed paper. Place 1 teaspoon hazelnut spread in center of each cookie. Top with remaining cookies; gently press together. Place cookies on a wire rack with waxed paper underneath.

In a small microwave-safe bowl, microwave chocolate chips on HIGH 1 minute or until chocolate softens; stir until smooth. Spoon into a resealable plastic bag. Snip off 1 corner of bag. Drizzle chocolate over cookies. Allow chocolate to harden.

Yield: about 2 dozen

CARAMEL-MACADAMIA NUT COOKIES

$1^1/_2$ cups macadamia nuts, coarsely chopped
    1   cup butter or margarine, softened
  $^3/_4$ cup firmly packed brown sugar
    1   egg
    1   tablespoon corn syrup
    1   teaspoon vanilla extract
    2   cups all-purpose flour

Spread macadamia nuts evenly on an ungreased baking sheet. Stirring occasionally, bake at 350° for 10 to 15 minutes or until nuts begin to brown. Remove from oven; cool to room temperature.

In a large bowl, cream butter and brown sugar until fluffy. Add eggs, corn syrup, and vanilla; stir until smooth. Add flour; stir until well blended. Fold in macadamia nuts. Drop tablespoonfuls of dough 2" apart onto a greased baking sheet. Bake in a preheated 350° oven for 10 to 12 minutes or until bottoms are golden brown. Cool on a wire rack.

Yield: about 3 dozen

"JUST FOR YOU"
Send your guests home with a box of tasty cookies. Place the cookies in the plain white treat box and then cover the box with bands of scrapbook paper and ribbon. Or completely cover the box with decorative paper before folding it into shape. Personalize the box with a coordinating chipboard monogram.

WATERMELON COOKIES

   5 cups all-purpose flour
   2 teaspoons baking powder
   1/2 teaspoon salt
   1 cup butter or margarine, softened
   1/3 cup vegetable oil
   1/3 cup butter-flavored shortening
   2 cups sugar
   2 eggs
   1 teaspoon lemon extract
   2 teaspoons dried lemon peel
     Green and red paste food coloring
   1 egg white, lightly beaten
   1 tube (4.25 ounces) black decorating
     icing with a set of decorating tips

In a large bowl, combine flour, baking powder, and salt. In another large bowl, beat butter, oil, shortening, and sugar until fluffy. Add eggs, lemon extract, and lemon peel; beat until smooth. Place 1 1/3 cups creamed mixture in a medium bowl; tint green. Tint remaining creamed mixture red. Add 1 2/3 cups flour mixture to green mixture; knead until a soft dough forms. Shape green dough into a ball and wrap in plastic wrap. Add remaining flour mixture to red mixture; knead until a soft dough forms. Shape into an 18" long roll; flatten roll on 1 side. Wrap in plastic wrap. Refrigerate both doughs 1 hour.

On a lightly floured surface, roll out green dough to a 3" x 18" rectangle. Brush curved side of red dough with egg white. Wrap green dough around curved side of red dough, trimming if necessary to fit. Wrap in plastic wrap and refrigerate 1 hour.

Slice dough into 1/4" thick slices. Place on a greased baking sheet. Bake in a preheated 350° oven for 10 to 12 minutes. Place on a wire rack to cool.

Using a small round decorating tip, pipe icing onto cookies to resemble seeds. Allow icing to harden.
Yield: about 5 1/2 dozen

SUMMERTIME TREATS
Celebrate the wonderfully warm days of summer with a box of watermelon cookies. Use the patterns (page 155) to cut a green rind, white border, and pink center for each watermelon. Glue the pieces together and add the "seeds." Print out labels on scrapbook paper. Place the cookies in a white treat box, adhere scrapbook paper, label, ribbon, and the watermelon. Tie the box closed. Your friends will fondly remember their first summer get-together.

SUMMERTIME
from Emma & Ellie

SUMMERTIME TREATS
from Emma & Ellie

CINNAMON-ALMOND MACAROONS

2¼ cups sliced almonds, toasted
½ teaspoon ground cinnamon
3 large egg whites
¾ cup superfine granulated sugar

Place almonds in a food processor; pulse process until coarsely chopped. Remove 3 tablespoons almonds; set aside. Add cinnamon to processor; process until almonds are finely ground.

In a medium bowl, beat egg whites until soft peaks form. Gradually add sugar, beating until mixture is very stiff. Gently fold ground almonds into egg white mixture.

Drop rounded teaspoonfuls of mixture 2" apart onto a parchment paper-lined baking sheet. Lightly sprinkle reserved chopped almonds onto tops of cookies. Bake in a preheated 350° oven for 14 to 15 minutes or until edges are lightly browned. Cool on parchment paper about 2 minutes; place on a wire rack to cool completely.
Yield: about 4 dozen

CHOCOLATE-KISSED COOKIES

1 package (16.5 ounces) refrigerated sugar cookie dough
1 package (8.5 ounces) milk chocolate candies with almonds

Drop 1 teaspoon cookie dough into each cup of an ungreased miniature muffin pan. Press chocolate candies into dough. Bake in a preheated 350° oven for 8 minutes or until edges are lightly browned. Cool in pan 5 minutes; place on a wire rack to cool completely.
Yield: about 4 dozen

COOKIE CANS
Decorate recycled cans with scrapbook paper, twill tape, and buttons before adding tissue paper and plastic-wrapped cookies. Make it personal by adhering travel stickers, ribbons, buttons, and letter tiles to a small envelope. Write your message on the layered cardstock tag inside.

DATE-FILLED PINWHEELS
COOKIES

- 1 cup butter or margarine, softened
- 1 cup granulated sugar
- 1 cup firmly packed brown sugar
- 3 eggs
- 1/2 teaspoon vanilla extract
- 3 1/2 cups all-purpose flour
- 1 teaspoon baking soda
- 1 teaspoon ground cinnamon
- 1/4 teaspoon salt

FILLING

- 12 ounces dates, finely chopped
- 6 tablespoons sugar
- 6 tablespoons orange juice
- 2 teaspoons grated orange zest

For cookies, beat butter and sugars until fluffy. Add eggs and vanilla; beat until smooth. In a medium bowl, combine dry ingredients and add to butter mixture; stir until a soft dough forms. Divide dough into fourths. Wrap in plastic wrap and chill 2 hours.

For filling, combine all ingredients in a heavy medium saucepan over medium heat. Stirring frequently, cook 8 minutes or until mixture thickens. Set aside.

On a well floured surface, roll out 1/4 of dough at a time to 1/8" thickness. Using a pastry wheel, cut dough into 2 1/2" squares; place 1" apart on a greased baking sheet. Use pastry wheel to make a 1" cut from each corner toward the center of each square. Place a heaping 1/2 teaspoonful of date mixture in center of each square. Bring every other dough corner toward the center, leaving filling uncovered; press into place at edge of filling. Chill 45 minutes.

Bake in a preheated 350° oven for 6 to 8 minutes or until edges are lightly browned. Place on a wire rack to cool.
Yield: about 6 dozen

PRETTY PINWHEELS

For an easy, breezy gift, line a fluted pie pan with a scrapbook paper circle that's been covered with clear, adhesive-backed shelf liner. Fill the pan with Date-Filled Pinwheels, wrap with a large cellophane piece, and tie with ribbon. For the paper pinwheel, cut diagonally into a 4" square of double-sided cardstock (don't cut all the way to the middle). Fold the points to the middle and secure with a colored brad. Glue the pinwheel to a clothespin and clip it to the cellophane.

CINNAMON-ORANGE BISCOTTI

- 1/2 cup butter or margarine, softened
- 1 cup sugar
- 3 eggs
- 1 tablespoon grated orange zest
- 1 teaspoon orange extract
- 3 cups all-purpose flour
- 1 teaspoon baking powder
- 1/2 teaspoon baking soda
- 1/2 teaspoon ground cinnamon
- 1/8 teaspoon salt

In a large bowl, beat butter and sugar until fluffy. Add eggs, orange zest, and orange extract; beat until smooth. In a medium bowl, combine flour, baking powder, baking soda, cinnamon, and salt. Add dry ingredients to butter mixture; stir until a soft dough forms.

Divide dough in half. On a greased and floured baking sheet, shape each piece of dough into a 2 1/2" x 10" loaf, flouring hands as necessary. Allowing 3" between loaves on baking sheet, bake in a preheated 375° oven for 25 to 28 minutes or until loaves are lightly browned; cool 10 minutes on baking sheet.

Cut loaves diagonally into 1/2" slices. Place slices flat on an ungreased baking sheet. Bake about 7 minutes or until lightly browned. Turn slices over and bake 6 to 8 minutes longer or until lightly browned. Place on a wire rack to cool.

Yield: about 2 1/2 dozen

AMARETTO BISCOTTI

- 1 package (6 ounces) zwieback toast
- 1/4 cup amaretto
- 6 ounces semisweet baking chocolate, chopped
- 1 tablespoon vegetable shortening
- 1 1/4 cups finely chopped pecans

Place pieces of toast on waxed paper. Spoon 1/2 teaspoon amaretto evenly over each piece; set aside.

Stirring constantly in a small saucepan, melt chocolate and shortening over low heat. Remove from heat. Holding each piece of toast over saucepan, spoon chocolate over one half. Roll chocolate-covered end in pecans. Return toast to waxed paper; allow chocolate to harden. Store in a cool, dry place.

Yield: about 2 dozen

CHEERY THANKS

Show your appreciation for a kind gesture with a coffee and biscotti basket. Cut the bird (patterns, page 150) from cardstock (a bit of machine sewing holds the wing in place) and use foam dots to attach to a layered $4\frac{5}{8}$"w x $5\frac{5}{8}$"h card (machine sew here too). Use rub-on letters for the "Thanks" ribbon flag. Staple ribbons to the card side and add a button and ribbon loop to the top. A unique fabric bag (just fold a 10" square of fabric in half and sew the bottom and one side), trimmed with beaded edging and ribbon, holds a bag of tasty biscotti.

TURTLE BROWNIES

BROWNIES
- 1 cup butter or margarine
- 4 ounces unsweetened baking chocolate
- 4 eggs
- 2 cups sugar
- 1 teaspoon vanilla-butter-nut flavoring
- 1½ cups all-purpose flour
- ½ teaspoon salt

TOPPING
- 1 package (14 ounces) caramels
- 2 tablespoons milk
- 1½ cups finely chopped toasted walnuts
- 1 cup semisweet chocolate chips
- 2 teaspoons vegetable shortening

For brownies, melt butter and chocolate in a double boiler over simmering water; remove from heat and allow to cool.

In a large bowl, lightly beat eggs. Add sugar and vanilla-butter-nut flavoring; beat until smooth. Combine chocolate mixture with sugar mixture. In a small bowl, combine flour and salt. Add dry ingredients to chocolate mixture; stir until smooth. Spread batter into 2 greased and floured 8" round baking pans. Bake in a preheated 350° oven for 20 to 25 minutes or until set in center. Place pans on a wire rack to cool.

For topping, place caramels and milk in a double boiler over medium heat. Stir until caramels melt. Stir in walnuts. Spoon caramel mixture over warm brownies, spreading evenly. Allow brownies to cool.

In a small microwave-safe bowl, microwave chocolate chips on HIGH 2 minutes, stirring after each minute. Add shortening; stir until well blended. Spread over caramel topping. Allow chocolate to harden. Cut into wedges. **Yield:** about 16 wedges, about 8 in each pan

CHOCOLATE RULES
Teacher hasn't had a blackboard like this before. Spray the lid of a tin with chalkboard paint and write your message with colored chalk. Add rub-on letters and numbers to the tin side and tie "ruler" ribbon around the tin. Use chalk to write on a black cardstock tag.

RASPBERRY CHOCOLATES

   6 ounces semisweet baking chocolate, chopped
   6 ounces white baking chocolate, chopped
  1/2 cup raspberry jelly

In separate small saucepans, melt chocolates over low heat, stirring constantly. Pour semisweet chocolate into a warm pie plate. Drizzle white chocolate over semisweet chocolate. Use the end of a wooden spoon to swirl together. Do not overmix. In batches, fill a bonbon mold half full with chocolate mixture. Using a small paintbrush, carefully brush chocolate mixture up sides of mold. Place mold in freezer 2 minutes or until chocolate hardens.

Spoon about 1/2 teaspoon raspberry jelly into each chocolate shell. Spoon a small amount of chocolate mixture over jelly, making sure edges are sealed. Return to freezer 2 minutes or until chocolate hardens. Invert and press on back of mold to release candies. Store in a cool place.
Yield: about 2 1/2 dozen

PEANUTTY CHOCOLATES

  1 bar (4.4 ounces) sweet chocolate
  1 cup peanut butter-flavored baking chips
  1/2 cup chopped roasted peanuts

Break chocolate into pieces and place in double boiler with baking chips. Melt over medium-low heat, stirring frequently. Remove from heat and spoon into miniature paper candy cups. Top with chopped peanuts. Refrigerate 30 minutes to set.
Yield: about 2 dozen

BE MY VALENTINE
Valentine chocolates are fun to make and give, especially in such a cute tin. Size and photocopy the vintage image (page 157) onto cardstock and cut out. Layer with scrapbook paper and glue to the tin top. A coordinating ribbon wraps around the tin.

STRAWBERRY SWEETHEART CAKES

Cakes are easier to slice if made ahead and chilled.

CAKES

1½	cups butter or margarine, softened
2	cups sugar
5	eggs, separated
1	tablespoon vanilla extract
½	cup strawberry ice cream topping
4½	cups sifted cake flour
4½	teaspoons baking powder
1	teaspoon salt
1¼	cups milk
¼	teaspoon red liquid food coloring

ICING

⅔	cup butter or margarine, softened
½	cup strawberry ice cream topping
¾	teaspoon vanilla extract
7	cups confectioners sugar
2	to 3 tablespoons milk
	Confectioners sugar to decorate

For cakes, grease each heart-shaped mold of a 6-mold baking pan (each mold is about 3¾" wide). In a large bowl, beat butter and sugar until fluffy. Add egg yolks and vanilla; beat until smooth. Beat in strawberry topping. In a medium bowl, combine cake flour, baking powder, and salt. Alternately add milk and dry ingredients to butter mixture; beat until well blended. Tint pink. In a medium bowl, beat egg whites until stiff. Fold into batter. Spoon about ¼ cup batter into each heart-shaped mold.

Bake in a preheated 350° oven for 11 to 13 minutes or until edges are lightly browned and a toothpick inserted in center of cake comes out clean. Cool in pan 5 minutes. Transfer cakes to a wire rack; cool completely. Chill cakes 2 hours before slicing.

For icing, beat butter, strawberry topping, and vanilla in a large bowl until well blended. Gradually add confectioners sugar and 2 tablespoons milk; beat until smooth. Add additional milk to icing, 1 teaspoon at a time, for desired consistency. Slice each cake in half horizontally. Spread about 1 rounded tablespoon icing between layers of each cake. Dust tops with confectioners sugar. Store in a single layer in a cool place.

Yield: about 3 dozen

PLAYING WITH THE QUEEN OF HEARTS

Love is in the air with these deliciously sweet cakes and the regal tag that holds a pin. To make the pin, cut a felt heart (pattern, page 157) and scallop one side. Embellish the heart with fabric, embroidery, flowers, ribbon, and a tiny cardstock heart sticker. Glue a pin back to the heart wrong side. Photocopy the Queen of Hearts playing card (page 157) onto cardstock. Knot a few ribbons through a hole in the top and pin the heart to the card.

EASTER GREETINGS

Look in the party section of the craft store for lots of great (and not just plain white!) food gift boxes. This windowed box is just the right size for one perfect Easter cupcake. Then look in the scrapbook section for crocheted circles, ribbon, wavy-edged scissors, jeweled brads, colorful paper and cardstock, and stickers. Combine these finds into a coordinating card to go with the cupcake.

EASTER CUPCAKES

1⅓ cups flaked coconut
     Green liquid food coloring
1   package (18.25 ounces) chocolate
     fudge cake mix
1⅓ cups water
3   eggs
⅓   cup vegetable oil
2   containers (16 ounces each) vanilla
     ready-to-spread frosting
     Vanilla wafers, graham cereal
     squares, and small pastel-colored
     jellybeans to decorate

Place coconut in a small bowl; tint light green.

In a medium bowl, combine cake mix, water, eggs, and oil. Beat at low speed of an electric mixer 30 seconds. Beat at medium speed 2 minutes. Fill greased and floured muffin cups about ⅔ full. Bake in a preheated 350° oven for 18 to 23 minutes or until a toothpick inserted in center of cupcake comes out clean. Cool in pan 5 minutes. Remove from pan and place on a wire rack to cool.

If necessary, use a serrated knife to level tops of cupcakes. Spread frosting on sides and tops of cupcakes. Press vanilla wafers or cereal pieces onto sides and sprinkle tinted coconut on tops. Place jellybeans on coconut.
Yield: about 2 dozen

JELLY BEAN CANDIED CORN

- 8 quarts popped white popcorn
- 12 ounces pastel jelly beans
- 3 cups sugar
- 1½ cups light corn syrup
- ¾ cup butter or margarine
- ½ cup water
- ½ teaspoon salt
- ½ teaspoon baking soda
- ⅛ teaspoon yellow liquid food coloring

Butter a large piece of aluminum foil; set aside.

Combine popcorn and jelly beans in a greased large roasting pan; set aside.

Butter sides of a 4½-quart Dutch oven. Combine sugar, corn syrup, butter, water, and salt in Dutch oven. Stirring constantly, cook over medium-low heat until sugar dissolves. Using a pastry brush dipped in hot water, wash down any sugar crystals on sides of pan. Attach a candy thermometer to pan, making sure thermometer does not touch bottom of pan.

Increase heat to medium-high and bring to a boil. Cook, without stirring, until mixture reaches soft-crack stage (approximately 280° to 290°). Test about ½ teaspoon mixture in ice water. Mixture will form hard threads in ice water but will soften when removed from the water. Remove from heat and stir in baking soda and food coloring. Pour over popcorn mixture; stir until well coated. Spread popcorn mixture on prepared foil to cool. Break into pieces.

Yield: about 36 cups

"EGGS-TRA" SPECIAL EASTER GOODIES

After the hunt for eggs is over, pass out Jelly Bean Candy Corn. Use decorative edge scissors to cut colorful gift sacks to 6" tall. Cut cardstock eggs (pattern, page 154) and trim with ribbons and rickrack; glue eggs to the sack fronts. Use more ribbons to decorate simple shipping tags. Place a bag of the candied corn in each sack and tie closed with yarn.

GARDEN CHICKEN CASSEROLE

- 2 cups chicken broth
- 2/3 cups sherry, divided
- 1 package (6 ounces) long grain and wild rice mix
- 1 small onion, chopped
- 2 small carrots, shredded
- 1 small green pepper, chopped
- 1/4 cup butter or margarine
- 3 cups diced cooked chicken
- 1 can (4 ounces) sliced mushrooms
- 1 package (8 ounces) cream cheese
- 8 ounces pasteurized process cheese, cut into pieces
- 1 cup evaporated milk
- 1/3 cup grated Parmesan cheese
- 1/2 cup sliced almonds

In a medium saucepan, bring broth and 1/3 cup sherry to a boil. Add contents of rice package, cover, and simmer over low heat 25 to 30 minutes or until all liquid is absorbed.

In a Dutch oven, sauté onion, carrots, and green pepper in butter until soft, about 5 minutes. Add rice, chicken, and mushrooms, mixing well. Place cream cheese, process cheese, and milk in a saucepan and melt over medium heat, stirring until smooth. Add to Dutch oven with remaining 1/3 cup sherry, mixing thoroughly. Pour into a buttered 9" x 13" baking dish. Top with Parmesan cheese and almonds. Cover and bake at 350° for 35 minutes; uncover and bake 15 minutes longer or until bubbly.
Yield: about 8 servings

Note: Casserole may be refrigerated overnight before baking. If refrigerated, increase baking time to 45 minutes covered and 15 minutes uncovered.

CASSEROLE COZY

Keep this fall casserole piping hot with this clever cozy made from 2 matching 19 1/2" x 14 1/2" place mats. Stack the place mats and topstitch together along the edges. Stitch 3" from each edge. Fold the carrier up along the stitched lines; to form each corner, stitch a line from the carrier edge to the inner stitched lines 2 1/2" from the pointed end. Fold the points toward the carrier long sides and sew on pretty wood buttons to hold the points in place.

CHEESY CORN CHOWDER

  2 cans (14³/₄ ounces each) yellow cream-style corn
  1 can (10³/₄ ounces) cream of potato soup, undiluted
  1 can (10³/₄ ounces) Cheddar cheese soup, undiluted
¹/₂ cup ready-to-use real bacon pieces
  2 cups milk
  2 teaspoons dried chopped onion
  1 teaspoon dried parsley flakes
¹/₄ teaspoon ground red pepper

In a large saucepan, combine all ingredients. Stirring occasionally, cook soup on medium heat until heated through. Store in refrigerator. **Yield:** about 7¹/₂ cups

FRIENDLY FALL PICNIC

This hearty soup is great for a fall outing. Place a fleece throw, plaid napkins, generous-sized bowls, and a thermos of chowder in an old-fashioned picnic basket. Decorate a tag with ribbon, brads, buttons, and rub-ons. Clip the tag to the basket and deliver some warmth to your friends.

MAPLE LEAVES

- 1 cup butter or margarine, softened
- 2/3 cup vegetable shortening
- 2 cups sugar
- 1/2 cup maple syrup
- 2 eggs
- 1 teaspoon maple flavoring
- 1 teaspoon vanilla extract
- 6 cups all-purpose flour
- 1/2 teaspoon salt
- 6 tablespoons water

  Orange, green, yellow, copper, brown, and red paste food coloring

In a large bowl, cream butter, shortening, and sugar until fluffy. Add syrup, eggs, maple flavoring, and vanilla; beat until smooth. In another large bowl, combine flour and salt. Add dry ingredients to creamed mixture; stir until a soft dough forms.

On a lightly floured surface, roll out dough to 1/4" thickness. Use a 3" x 2 1/2" maple leaf-shaped cookie cutter to cut out cookies. Transfer to a greased baking sheet. Bake in a preheated 350° oven for 7 to 9 minutes or until bottoms are lightly browned. Transfer cookies to a wire rack to cool.

Place 1 tablespoon water in each of 6 small bowls. Tint each bowl of water with a small amount of food coloring. To color cookies, use a small paintbrush to lightly brush diluted food coloring onto cookies to resemble fall leaves. Allow to dry.
Yield: about 9 dozen

MAPLE LEAF TOTE
A thermos of hot cider and a bag full of Maple Leaf Cookies are a sweet treat on a blustery day. Use the leaf cookie cutter to make fusible fabric appliqués (page 143). Fuse the appliqués to a small canvas tote bag, sew on a few buttons, and tie a tag to the handles after adding the cookies to the bag.

JACK-O'-LANTERN SUGARLESS COOKIES

- ³/₄ cup all-purpose flour
- ¹/₂ teaspoon baking powder
- 1 egg
- ¹/₄ cup margarine, softened
- ¹/₂ teaspoon vanilla extract, divided
  Orange paste food coloring
- 14 packets artifical sweetener, divided
- ¹/₄ cup water
- 1 tablespoon margarine, softened
- 2 tablespoons cream cheese, softened
- 1 tablespoon cocoa

In a large mixing bowl, combine flour and baking powder. Add egg, ¹/₄ cup margarine, and ¹/₄ teaspoon vanilla; stir until well blended. Add paste food coloring to dough, thoroughly working in color until well distributed and dough is desired shade.

On a lightly floured surface, roll out dough to ¹/₄" thickness. Using a 1¹/₂" round cookie cutter, cut out dough. Place cookies on ungreased baking sheet and bake in a preheated 350° oven for 12 to 15 minutes or until firm to touch. While cookies are baking, combine 7 sweetener packets with water. After baking, use a pastry brush to brush sweetener mixture on warm cookies.

For icing, combine remaining 7 sweetener packets with margarine, cream cheese, and cocoa. Place icing in pastry bag fitted with a small round tip. Pipe faces on cookies.
Yield: about 3 dozen

COOKIE CONES
Wrap "boo-tiful" scrapbook paper into a cone shape and tape together. Glue jumbo rickrack and tiny trim along the top edge. Photocopy a spooky image (page 156) and glue to a layered cardstock tag. A colored brad attaches the tag to the cone. Line the cone with tissue paper before adding the cookies.

HAIRY MONSTERS

- 1/2 cup butter or margarine
- 3/4 cup sugar
- 1 egg
- 1 cup chopped dates
- 2 cups crispy rice cereal
- 1 cup coarsely chopped salted peanuts
- 1 teaspoon vanilla extract
- 1 1/3 cups sweetened finely shredded coconut

Whisking constantly, combine butter, sugar, and egg in a heavy medium skillet over medium heat. Add dates to butter mixture. Continue to cook and whisk mixture about 10 minutes, mashing as dates soften. Remove from heat; stir in cereal, peanuts, and vanilla.

When mixture is cool enough to handle, use greased hands to shape into 1" balls; roll in coconut. Cool.

Yield: about 4 dozen

ORANGE SLICE COOKIES

- 3/4 cup butter or margarine, softened
- 1 cup granulated sugar
- 1/2 cup firmly packed brown sugar
- 1 egg
- 1 teaspoon vanilla extract
- 1 3/4 cups all-purpose flour
- 1/2 teaspoon baking powder
- 1/2 teaspoon salt
- 2 cups orange slice gumdrop candies, quartered

In a large bowl, cream butter and sugars until fluffy. Add egg and vanilla; beat until smooth. In a small bowl, combine flour, baking powder, and salt. Add dry ingredients to creamed mixture; stir until a soft dough forms. Stir in candy pieces. Shape dough into three 9" long rolls. Wrap in plastic wrap and chill 3 hours or until firm enough to handle.

Cut dough into 1/4" thick slices. Place 1" apart on lightly greased baking sheets. Bake in a preheated 375° oven for 6 to 8 minutes or until edges are lightly browned. Cool cookies on wire racks.

Yield: about 6 dozen

HALLOWEEN TREAT BAGS

Send the kids home from the Halloween party with their own spooky sack of goodies. Place a few stacks of cookies in treat bags and secure with ribbon and a painted mini clothespin. Personalize with a Jack-O'-Lantern stamped and layered tag.

CARAMEL CRACKERS

- 1 package (12.25 ounces) small round buttery crackers
- 1 cup dry-roasted peanuts
- 1 cup sugar
- 1/2 cup butter or margarine
- 1/2 cup light corn syrup
- 1 teaspoon vanilla extract
- 1 teaspoon baking soda

Combine crackers and peanuts in a greased large shallow baking pan. In a saucepan, bring sugar, butter, and corn syrup to a boil and cook 5 minutes. Remove from heat; stir in vanilla and baking soda. Pour caramel mixture over crackers and peanuts; stir well.

Bake at 350° for 1 hour, stirring every 15 minutes. Pour onto waxed paper and break apart; allow to cool.
Yield: about 7 1/2 cups

CINNAMON-APPLE POPCORN

- 2 cups chopped dried apples
- 10 cups popped popcorn
- 2 cups pecan halves
- 4 tablespoons butter, melted
- 2 tablespoons firmly packed brown sugar
- 1 teaspoon ground cinnamon
- 1/4 teaspoon ground nutmeg
- 1/4 teaspoon vanilla extract

Place apples in a large shallow baking pan. Bake at 250° for 20 minutes. Remove pan from oven and stir in popcorn and pecans. In a small bowl, combine remaining ingredients. Drizzle butter mixture over popcorn mixture, stirring well.

Bake 30 minutes longer at 250°, stirring every 10 minutes. Pour onto waxed paper to cool.
Yield: about 14 cups

CARAMEL CORN PUFFS

- 1 package (12.5 ounces) puffed corn cereal
- 1 cup pecan halves
- 1 cup sugar
- 1/2 cup butter or margarine
- 1/2 cup light corn syrup
- 1 teaspoon vanilla extract
- 1 teaspoon baking soda

Combine cereal and pecans in a greased large shallow baking pan. In a saucepan, bring sugar, butter, and corn syrup to a boil and cook 5 minutes. Remove from heat; stir in vanilla and baking soda. Pour caramel mixture over cereal and pecans; stir well.

Bake at 250° for 1 hour, stirring every 15 minutes. Pour onto waxed paper and break apart; allow to cool.
Yield: about 10 cups

CHRISTMAS SNACKS

A plain canister of snack mix takes on a merry appearance when wrapped with a paper band and trimmed with a personalized tag. Ribbon, cord, and bells tied to the lid celebrate the season.

O CHRISTMAS TREE

Your friends will remember the sweet spiciness of these cookies each time they see this festive felt ornament. Use the larger cookie cutter to cut 2 felt trees. Punch felt "ornaments" with a ¼" hole punch. Use embroidery floss *French Knots* (page 144) to attach the ornaments to a felt tree. *Straight Stitches* anchor the ribbon garland. Wrap a bangle bracelet (with loops) with the same ribbon and sew felt ornaments to the loops. Placing the bracelet in between, glue the felt trees together. With the cookies inside, fold over the bag top and wrap with jumbo rickrack. Cut slits in the bag top and tie on the ornament with a coordinating ribbon.

SPICY CHRISTMAS TREES

COOKIES

- $^1/_3$ cup butter or margarine, softened
- $^1/_3$ cup vegetable shortening
- $1^1/_4$ cups sugar
- 1 cup sour cream
- $^1/_2$ cup molasses
- 2 eggs
- 1 teaspoon vanilla extract
- $5^1/_4$ cups all-purpose flour
- $^1/_4$ cup cocoa
- 1 tablespoon ground cinnamon
- 2 teaspoons baking powder
- 2 teaspoons ground ginger
- 1 teaspoon ground allspice
- 1 teaspoon baking soda
- 1 teaspoon salt

ICING

- 1 cup confectioners sugar
- 1 tablespoon plus 1 teaspoon milk

For cookies, beat butter, shortening, and sugar in a large bowl until fluffy. Add sour cream, molasses, eggs, and vanilla; beat until smooth. In another large bowl, combine flour, cocoa, cinnamon, baking powder, ginger, allspice, baking soda, and salt. Add half of dry ingredients to butter mixture; stir until a soft dough forms. Stir remaining dry ingredients, 1 cup at a time, into dough; use hands if necessary to mix well. Divide dough into fourths. Wrap in plastic wrap and chill 2 hours or until dough is firm.

On a lightly floured surface, roll out $^1/_4$ of dough to slightly less than $^1/_4$" thickness. Use $3^1/_4$" x 4" and $2^1/_4$" x $3^1/_4$" Christmas tree-shaped cookie cutters to cut out cookies. Transfer to a greased baking sheet. Bake in a preheated 350° oven for 7 to 9 minutes or until firm to the touch. Transfer cookies to a wire rack. Repeat with remaining dough.

For icing, combine confectioners sugar and milk in a small bowl; stir until smooth. Spoon icing into a pastry bag fitted with a small round tip. Pipe outline onto each cookie. Allow icing to harden.

Yield: about 7 dozen

HOLIDAY CHERRY CAKES

- 1 package (18¹/₄ ounces) cherry cake mix
- 1 package (3.4 ounces) vanilla instant pudding mix
- 4 eggs
- 1 cup water
- ¹/₃ cup vegetable oil
- 1 container (8 ounces) red candied cherries, chopped
- 4¹/₂ to 4³/₄ cups confectioners sugar
- 7 tablespoons milk
- 3 tablespoons vegetable shortening
- 2 tablespoons light corn syrup
- 1 teaspoon clear vanilla extract
- 2 tubes (4.25 ounces each) green and red decorating icing

In a large bowl, combine cake mix, pudding mix, eggs, water, and oil; beat 2 minutes or until smooth. Stir in cherries. Spoon ¹/₂ cup batter into each greased mold of a 6-mold fluted tube pan. Bake in a preheated 350° oven for 20 to 23 minutes or until a toothpick inserted in center of cake comes out clean. Cool in pan 5 minutes. Remove from pan and cool completely on a wire rack.

In a large bowl, combine confectioners sugar, milk, shortening, corn syrup, and vanilla; beat until smooth. Spoon white icing over tops of cakes; allow icing to harden. Transfer red and green icing into pastry bags. Use green icing and a small leaf tip to pipe holly leaves onto cakes. Use red icing and a small round tip to pipe berries onto cakes; allow icing to harden.
Yield: about 2 dozen

HOLLY JOLLY DESSERTS
Mini cakes are quite festive when presented under glass, especially when the tag encourages your guests to wish for what their hearts desire. Dress up a cardstock tag with chipboard letters, ribbon, glitter, felt rounds, and little painted wood holly sprigs. Use a curly ornament hanger to attach the tag to the cake pedestal.

FRUIT MUESLI BARS

1 package (18.25 ounces) yellow cake mix
1/2 cup firmly packed brown sugar
3/4 cup butter or margarine, softened
1 1/2 cups muesli cereal
1 jar (12 ounces) strawberry preserves

Combine cake mix and brown sugar in a large bowl; use a pastry blender to cut in butter. Stir in cereal. Reserving 1 1/2 cups of mixture, press remaining cereal mixture into an ungreased 9" x 13" baking pan. Spread preserves over crust almost to edges of pan. Sprinkle remaining cereal mixture over preserves.

Bake at 350° for 35 to 38 minutes or until top is lightly browned. Cool in pan on a wire rack. Cut into 1" x 2" bars.
Yield: about 4 dozen

AUSTRIAN LINZER BARS

1 cup butter or margarine, softened
3/4 cup sugar
2 egg yolks
1 tablespoon grated lemon zest
1 teaspoon vanilla extract
2 cups all-purpose flour
1 teaspoon ground cinnamon
1/2 teaspoon baking powder
1/2 teaspoon ground allspice
1 cup sliced almonds, finely ground
1 cup seedless raspberry jam
1 cup sliced almonds, coarsely chopped

In a large bowl, cream butter and sugar until fluffy. Add egg yolks, lemon zest, and vanilla; beat until smooth. In a small bowl, combine flour, cinnamon, baking powder, and allspice. Add dry ingredients to creamed mixture; stir until a soft dough forms. Stir in ground almonds.

Press dough into a greased 9" x 13" baking pan. Spread raspberry jam over dough. Sprinkle coarsely chopped almonds over jam.

Bake at 375° for 28 to 30 minutes or until edges are browned. Cool in pan. Cut into 1" x 2" bars.
Yield: about 4 dozen

WINTERY DESSERT BARS

Be the hit of the cookie exchange party with these dessert bars. Bring the bars to the party on a clear glass plate which has been placed on a purchased decorative-edge charger. Wrap in cellophane and tie closed. Layer and glue punched snowflake shapes together; then, glue to a painted clothespin. Add a sparkly jewel to the snowflake center before clipping to the cellophane.

CHILL CHASERS

Keep these little snowman mugs and mats on hand for last minute Christmas gifts. Decorate a super jumbo bottle cap (available at scrapbook stores) with scrapbook paper or cardstock, ribbon, punched shapes, and glitter. Add a handwritten message before gluing the paper in the cap. Glue a clothespin to the cap back. Fill a mug with bagged mocha or cocoa mix. Place the mug on a coiled rag coaster (page 146) and wrap both in cellophane. Clip the bottle cap to the cellophane.

MALTED COCOA MIX

- 1 package (25.6 ounces) nonfat dry milk powder
- 6 cups miniature marshmallows
- 1 container (16 ounces) instant cocoa mix for milk
- 1 jar (13 ounces) malted milk powder
- 1 cup confectioners sugar
- 1 jar (6 ounces) non-dairy powdered creamer
- $1/2$ teaspoon salt

In a very large bowl, combine dry milk, marshmallows, cocoa mix, malted milk powder, confectioners sugar, creamer, and salt; stir until well blended. Store in a resealable plastic bag. Give with serving instructions.
Yield: about 20 cups mix

To serve: Pour 6 ounces hot water over $1/3$ cup cocoa mix; stir until well blended.

HAZELNUT MOCHA MIX

- 1 package (25.6 ounces) nonfat dry milk powder
- 1 package (16 ounces) confectioners sugar
- 1 package (15 ounces) chocolate mix for milk
- 1 jar (11 ounces) non-dairy powdered creamer
- 1 jar (15 ounces) hazelnut-flavored non-dairy powdered creamer
- $1/2$ cup cocoa
- $1/4$ cup instant coffee granules

In a very large bowl, combine dry milk, confectioners sugar, chocolate mix, creamers, cocoa, and coffee granules; stir until well blended. Store in a resealable plastic bag. Give with serving instructions.
Yield: about $18 1/4$ cups mix

To serve: Pour 6 ounces hot water over 3 tablespoons mix; stir until well blended.

FRUIT FIESTA PIZZA

- $\frac{1}{2}$ of a 16.5-ounce tube package refrigerated sugar cookie dough
- 1 package (8 ounces) cream cheese, softened
- $\frac{1}{3}$ cup sugar
- 2 tablespoons plus 2 teaspoons orange-flavored liqueur, divided
- $\frac{1}{2}$ teaspoon vanilla extract
- 4 cups total sliced fresh apricots, strawberries, bananas, and whole blueberries
- $\frac{1}{4}$ cup apricot preserves

Press cookie dough into a greased 12" pizza pan. Bake in a preheated 350° oven for 12 to 15 minutes or until dough is lightly browned. Cool pan on a wire rack.

In a medium bowl, beat cream cheese, sugar, 2 tablespoons liqueur, and vanilla until fluffy. Spread over cooled crust. Beginning at outer edge, arrange fruit slices over cream cheese mixture. Melt apricot preserves in a small saucepan over low heat. Remove from heat. Stir in remaining 2 teaspoons liqueur. Brush over fruit. Cover and chill 30 minutes. Cut into wedges to serve.

Yield: about 12 servings

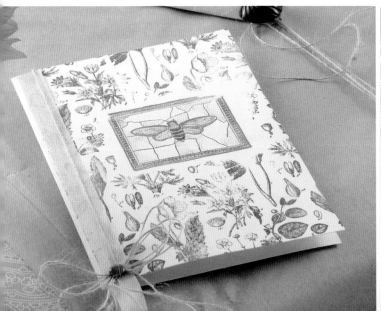

SPECIAL DELIVERY

What could be hidden under the plain brown wrapper? Why it's a Fruit Fiesta Pizza! Ask your local pizzeria for a pizza box and wrap in brown paper (wrap the box the opposite way you'd normally wrap a gift—you don't want to turn the pizza upside down!). Tie with jute twine and add a button. To stamp the card front background, cut a sticky note to the size of the area to be left unstamped and adhere to the background rubber stamp. Ink the image, remove the sticky note, and stamp on the card. Stamp the focal image in the blank space and color with pencils. Add a delicate ribbon, thin jute twine, and a brad along the inside edge of the card, and you've got a great "Just Because" gift.

PIÑA COLADA PIE

- 1 package (3.4 ounces) vanilla instant pudding mix
- 1½ cups liquid piña colada drink mix, chilled
- 1 package (8 ounces) cream cheese, softened
- 1 can (15¼ ounces) pineapple tidbits, drained
- ¼ cup finely shredded coconut
- 1 graham cracker pie crust (6 ounces)
- Garnish: kiwi fruit slices

In a medium bowl, add pudding mix to drink mix; beat until thickened. Add cream cheese; beat until smooth. Stir in pineapple and coconut. Spoon into crust. Cover and chill until set.

Garnish, if desired.

Yield: about 8 servings

CREAMY STRAWBERRY PIE

- 1 package (10 ounces) marshmallows
- 1 package (16 ounces) frozen whole strawberries, thawed and drained
- 3 tablespoons strawberry liqueur or strawberry juice
- 1 cup whipping cream, whipped
- 1 large (9 ounces) graham cracker pie crust
- Garnish: fresh strawberries

Place marshmallows in a medium microwave-safe bowl. Microwave on HIGH 1½ to 2 minutes or until marshmallows melt, stirring every 30 seconds. Beat in strawberries and liqueur. Fold in whipped cream. Spoon into crust. Cover and chill until set.

Garnish, if desired.

Yield: about 10 servings

CLEARLY DELICIOUS!

An inexpensive clear pie container holds a yummy treat. Coordinating scrapbook paper and cardstock circles decorate the lid, while a twill tape tie keeps the container closed. Tell the recipient your feelings about the pie on a layered gift tag.

SAUCY JAR & TAG

The rich flavor of Apple Spice Cake is enhanced with a warm applesauce topping. Place the topping in a jar. Make a perky paper and felt posy (with a fabric brad center) and attach to a twill tape length. Add a rub-on message and tie the tape around a fabric skirt placed on the topping jar. A hand-lettered and layered scrapbook paper tag completes the gift nicely.

APPLE SPICE CAKE

CAKE

- 1 package (18.25 ounces) spice cake mix
- 1/2 cup applesauce
- 4 eggs
- 1/3 cup vegetable oil
- 1 teaspoon maple flavoring
- 2 cups cored, unpeeled, and chopped Granny Smith apples (about 2 large apples)

TOPPING

- 1 cup applesauce
- 2/3 cup firmly packed brown sugar
- 1/2 cup butter or margarine

For cake, combine cake mix, eggs, applesauce, oil, and maple flavoring in a large bowl. Beat at low speed of an electric mixer 30 seconds. Beat at medium speed 2 minutes. Stir in apples. Pour batter into a greased and floured 10" fluted tube pan. Bake in a preheated 350° oven for 40 to 45 minutes or until a toothpick inserted in cake comes out clean. Cool in pan 10 minutes. Invert onto a serving plate and cool completely.

For topping, combine all ingredients in a small saucepan over medium-high heat. Stirring frequently, bring to a boil; reduce heat and cook until thickened. Cool and pour into a container with lid. Give topping with cake. Give with serving instructions.

Yield: about 16 servings

To serve: Reheat topping and serve over cake.

KEY LIME PIE

9"	frozen pie crust, thawed
4	egg yolks
1	can (14 ounces) sweetened condensed milk
1/3	cup freshly squeezed lime juice (juice of about 3 limes)
	Green food coloring (optional)
4	egg whites
1/2	teaspoon cream of tartar
1/2	cup sugar

Prick crust with a fork. Bake in a preheated 450° oven for 8 minutes. Cool completely on a wire rack.

Combine egg yolks, condensed milk, and lime juice in a medium saucepan over low heat. Attach a cooking thermometer to pan, making sure thermometer does not touch bottom of pan. Cook, stirring constantly, until mixture reaches 160° (about 10 minutes). Remove from heat. If desired, tint green.

Beat egg whites and cream of tartar in a large bowl until foamy using highest speed of an electric mixer. Gradually add sugar; beat until stiff peaks form.

Pour filling into crust. Spread meringue evenly over filling, sealing to edge. Bake at 325° for 25 to 30 minutes or until meringue is lightly browned. Cool completely on a wire rack. Cover and store in refrigerator.

Yield: 8 to 10 servings

PIE TO GO

The fresh cool color of Key Lime Pie is reflected in the pie box packaging. Just wrap a cake box with dotted ribbon, tie the box closed with a thinner trim, and add lime green stamped and layered scrapbook paper ovals on top. Form a flower by gathering one edge of a ribbon length; glue a button to the center. Glue the flower to the box, along with layered paper leaves (pattern, page 151).

ROCKY ROAD TART
CRUST

1	cup sugar
1	cup all-purpose flour
1	cup finely ground almonds
1	teaspoon baking powder
$1/2$	cup butter or margarine
2	ounces unsweetened chocolate
1	teaspoon vanilla extract

FILLING

6	ounces cream cheese, softened
$1/2$	cup sugar
$1/4$	cup butter or margarine, softened
2	tablespoons all-purpose flour
1	egg
$1/2$	teaspoon vanilla extract
$1/2$	cup slivered almonds
1	cup (6 ounces) semisweet chocolate chips
2	cups miniature marshmallows

For crust, combine sugar, flour, ground almonds, and baking powder in a medium bowl. In a small saucepan, melt butter and chocolate over low heat, stirring until smooth. Add chocolate mixture and vanilla to dry ingredients; stir until dough is crumbly. Press evenly into bottom of a greased and floured 9" springform pan.

For filling, beat cream cheese, sugar, and butter in a medium bowl until fluffy. Beat in flour, egg, and vanilla. Fold in almonds and chocolate chips. Spoon batter evenly over crust.

Bake at 350° for 40 to 45 minutes or until a toothpick inserted in center comes out clean. Sprinkle marshmallows evenly over top. Bake 4 to 5 minutes longer or until marshmallows are lightly browned. Cool in pan 10 minutes. Remove sides of pan; cool completely.
Yield: 8 to 10 servings

PRALINE TEA CAKES

CAKES

- 1 cup butter or margarine, softened
- 1 cup sugar
- 6 eggs
- 1 teaspoon maple-flavored extract
- 1 cup finely crushed vanilla wafer cookies
- 1 teaspoon baking powder
- 1/2 teaspoon salt
- 1/2 teaspoon dried orange peel

TOPPING

- 2 cups chopped pecans, toasted
- 1 cup butter or margarine
- 1 cup firmly packed brown sugar

For cakes, beat butter and sugar in a large bowl until fluffy. Add eggs and maple extract; beat until smooth. Add remaining ingredients; stir until well blended. Pour batter evenly into 12 greased and floured shortcake tins. Bake in a preheated 350° oven for 15 to 20 minutes or until a toothpick inserted in center comes out clean. Cool in pan 10 minutes; invert onto a wire rack to cool completely.

For topping, combine butter and sugar in a medium saucepan over medium heat. Stirring constantly, bring to a boil and cook 2 to 3 minutes or until mixture thickens. Stir in pecans. Spoon about 2 tablespoons topping into center of each cake. Allow to cool. **Yield:** 1 dozen

TEA TIME DAINTIES

A pretty mini basket becomes the perfect nest for a pair of delicious tea cakes. Weave a delicate ribbon through the basket rim and tie a bow in the corner. Glue a mini tag to a vintage button and clip to some tea bags that have a decorative paper topper. Add the tea cakes and pop over to your friend's house to enjoy a special chat.

BUTTERSCOTCH COFFEE CAKE

- 1 package (25 ounces) frozen white dinner rolls
- 1/2 cup sugar
- 1 package (3.5 ounces) butterscotch pudding and pie filling mix
- 1 tablespoon ground cinnamon
- 1/2 cup butter or margarine, melted
- 1 cup chopped pecans

Place frozen rolls in bottom of a greased 12-cup fluted tube pan. In a small bowl, combine sugar, pudding mix, and cinnamon. Sprinkle sugar mixture over rolls. Pour butter over sugar mixture. Sprinkle pecans on top. Cover with plastic wrap and let rise in a warm place (80° to 85°) 5 1/2 to 6 1/2 hours or until doubled in size. To serve in early morning, coffee cake can rise overnight (about 8 hours).

Bake in a preheated 350° oven for 30 to 35 minutes or until brown. Remove from oven and immediately invert onto serving plate. Serve warm.
Yield: about 16 servings

BOXED & BEAUTIFUL

An elegantly wrapped box conceals an equally elegant coffee cake. Just wrap a cake box with a wrapping paper band and tie with a satin, multi-loop bow. Print a gorgeous monogram on textured cardstock and insert it in a small frame that can be tied to the bow.

HOSTESS APRON

Give an apron, along with a yummy dessert, to the hostess with the mostess. Add rickrack to the bottom edge of a hemmed 22" x 9" fabric pocket. Topstitch the pocket fabric to a 28" x 18" dish towel along the bottom and side edges. Create 3 pocket sections by stitching about 7" in from each side. Center a 72" ribbon length along the apron top edge and topstitch in place.

NUTTY CARAMEL APPLE DESSERT

This is good with a scoop of vanilla ice cream.

- 1½ cups all-purpose flour
- 1 teaspoon baking powder
- ½ teaspoon apple pie spice
- ¼ teaspoon salt
- 1½ cups quick-cooking oats
- 1 cup firmly packed brown sugar
- ¾ cup chilled butter or margarine
- 1 can (20 ounces) sliced apples, drained and coarsely chopped
- 1 cup chopped walnuts
- 1 jar (12 ounces) caramel ice cream topping

In a medium bowl, combine flour, baking powder, apple pie spice, and salt. Stir in oats and brown sugar. Using a pastry blender or 2 knives, cut in butter until mixture is well blended. Reserve 1 cup oat mixture. Press remaining oat mixture into bottom of a lightly greased 9" square baking dish. Layer apples, reserved oat mixture, and walnuts. Drizzle with ice cream topping.

Bake in a preheated 375° oven for 25 to 30 minutes or until lightly browned and a toothpick inserted into cake portion comes out clean. Cool in pan on a wire rack. Cover and store in a cool place. Give with serving instructions.

Yield: about 12 servings

To serve: Uncover and bake in a preheated 325° oven 25 minutes or until heated through. Serve warm.

THE GIFT OF PIE

What dessert lover wouldn't appreciate his own little pie? Cover individual cake boxes with scrapbook paper or cardstock, layering two coordinating papers around the window. Place the pie inside the box and tie with a soft ribbon. Punch a motif from one paper and glue to a tag made from the coordinating paper.

CRUNCHY PEANUT BUTTER PIES
CRUST
- 1/2 cup butter or margarine, melted
- 1¼ cups graham cracker crumbs
- 1/4 cup sugar

FILLING
- 1 package (8 ounces) cream cheese, softened
- 2 cups confectioners sugar
- 3/4 cup crunchy peanut butter
- 1 cup milk
- 1 container (8 ounces) frozen non-dairy whipped topping, thawed
- 1/2 cup chopped peanuts

For crust, combine butter, graham cracker crumbs, and sugar; stir until mixture is crumbly. Press evenly into six 5" pie pans. Bake at 350° for 6 minutes; cool.

For filling, beat cream cheese in a large bowl until fluffy. Add confectioners sugar and peanut butter, beating until well blended. Gradually stir in milk. Fold whipped topping into cream cheese mixture; spoon into crusts. Sprinkle with chopped peanuts. Freeze until firm.

Place in refrigerator about 30 minutes before serving.
Yield: 6

BLUEBERRY-LEMON PIES
CRUST
- 1/2 cup butter or margarine, melted
- 1¼ cups graham cracker crumbs
- 1/4 cup sugar

FILLING
- 1 can (14 ounces) sweetened condensed milk
- 1 can (6 ounces) frozen lemonade concentrate, thawed
- 1 container (8 ounces) frozen non-dairy whipped topping, thawed
- 6 tablespoons canned blueberry pie filling, chilled
- Garnish: lemon zest strips

For crust, combine butter, graham cracker crumbs, and sugar; stir until mixture is crumbly. Press evenly into six 5" pie pans. Bake at 350° for 6 minutes; cool.

For filling, combine sweetened condensed milk and lemonade concentrate in a medium bowl. Fold in whipped topping. Spoon lemon mixture into crusts. Cover and chill.

Top each tart with 1 tablespoon chilled pie filling. Garnish, if desired.
Yield: 6

Sauces, Mixes, & Jams—Oh My!

CRANBERRY MUSTARD

- 2/3 cup finely chopped onion
- 2 tablespoons vegetable oil
- 6 tablespoons firmly packed brown sugar
- 2 teaspoons grated orange zest
- 2 cans (14 ounces each) whole berry cranberry sauce
- 2/3 cup prepared mustard

In a large skillet over medium heat, sauté onion in oil about 5 minutes or until onion is tender. Add brown sugar and orange zest. Stirring frequently, cook about 1 minute or until sugar dissolves. Add cranberry sauce and mustard; stir until well blended. Remove from heat and cool.

Serve at room temperature as a condiment or use as a sauce for grilling. Store in refrigerator.

Yield: about 4¼ cups

SPICY ONION CHUTNEY

- 1/3 cup unsalted butter or margarine
- 1 cup firmly packed brown sugar
- 6 cups chopped onions (about 3 pounds onions)
- 3 cloves garlic, minced
- 1/2 cup orange juice
- 1/4 cup apple cider vinegar
- 2 tablespoons grated orange zest
- 6 whole cloves

Melt butter in a heavy Dutch oven over medium heat. Add brown sugar; stirring constantly until sugar dissolves. Cook 2 to 3 minutes or until sugar begins to caramelize. Add onions and garlic (sugar may harden a little); stirring constantly, cook about 10 minutes or until onions are tender. Stir in orange juice, vinegar, orange zest, and cloves; cook about 20 minutes or until mixture thickens.

Serve warm as a condiment with meat, breads, or vegetables. Store in refrigerator.

Yield: about 3 cups

HOMEMADE GOODNESS

Need a quick hostess gift? Photocopy the label (page 153) onto patterned cardstock and adhere to a jar of easy-to-make chutney or mustard. A coordinating cardstock circle covers the lid.

homemade
Cranberry
Mustard

homemade
Spicy Onion
Chutney

VERY STRAWBERRY SAUCE

2 tablespoons cornstarch
1/4 cup water
1 jar (12 ounces) strawberry preserves
1 package (10 ounces) frozen sweetened sliced strawberries, thawed
1/2 cup sugar

In a small bowl, dissolve cornstarch in water. Combine preserves, strawberries, and sugar in a medium saucepan over medium-high heat; stir until well blended. Stir cornstarch mixture into fruit mixture. Stirring constantly, boil about 5 minutes or until mixture thickens.

Cool and store in refrigerator. Serve warm or cold.
Yield: about 2 1/2 cups

CRUNCHY WALNUT SAUCE

1/2 cup firmly packed brown sugar
1 tablespoon cornstarch
1 cup boiling water
1 cup finely chopped walnuts, toasted
1 tablespoon butter
Dash of salt
1 teaspoon butter flavoring

Combine brown sugar and cornstarch in a heavy medium saucepan. Stirring constantly over medium heat, gradually add boiling water. Add walnuts, butter, and salt; cook about 6 minutes or until mixture thickens. Remove from heat. Stir in butter flavoring.

Cool and store in refrigerator. Serve warm.
Yield: about 1 1/3 cups

CHOCOLATE SATIN SYRUP

1 cup sugar
1/2 cup cocoa
1/4 teaspoon salt
1 cup light corn syrup
1/2 cup half and half
3 tablespoons butter or margarine
1 teaspoon vanilla extract

In a heavy medium saucepan, combine sugar, cocoa, and salt. Add corn syrup, half and half, and butter. Stirring constantly, cook over medium heat 5 to 7 minutes or until sugar dissolves. Remove from heat; stir in vanilla.

Cool and store in refrigerator. Serve warm or cold.
Yield: about 2 2/3 cups

ICE CREAM SUNDAE KIT
An ice cream sundae kit is a big hit on hot summer days. Assorted sprinkles and nuts, along with yummy sauces and perfect parfait glasses are so inviting on a scrapbook paper-lined tray. Finish off this sweet treat with coordinating labels and rickrack trim on the jar lids.

SNAPPY STRAWBERRY-JALAPEÑO SAUCE

2 jars (18 ounces each) strawberry
   preserves
1 jar (12 ounces) pickled jalapeño
   pepper slices, drained

Pulse process preserves and jalapeño slices in a food processor until peppers are finely chopped. Pour into jars; cover and store in refrigerator. Give with serving instructions.
Yield: about 4 cups

To serve: In a medium bowl, combine 8 ounces softened cream cheese and 8 ounces finely shredded sharp Cheddar cheese; beat until well blended. Spread into a serving dish. Spoon 1 cup sauce over cheese. Serve with crackers.

TOASTED PECAN-PEPPER JAM

3 cups chopped sweet red peppers
$^1/_2$ cup apple cider vinegar
1 package ($1^3/_4$ ounces) powdered fruit
   pectin
$4^1/_2$ cups sugar
1 cup finely chopped pecans, toasted
   Crackers to serve

Process peppers in a food processor until finely chopped. In a Dutch oven, combine peppers, vinegar, and pectin over medium-high heat. Bring to a rolling boil. Add sugar. Stirring constantly, bring to a rolling boil again and boil 1 minute. Stir in pecans. Remove from heat; skim off foam. Spoon jam into heat-resistant jars; cover and cool to room temperature. Store in refrigerator. Serve with crackers.
Yield: about $5^1/_2$ cups

PEPPERY GIFT BASKET

A peppery sauce and jam remind of us days gone by, as do these mini crocheted granny squares we found at the flea market. They make the perfect liner for our small basket of sauce and jam. Sew the squares together to fit in the basket, add twill tape and buttons at the sides, and place in the basket. Add colorful scrapbook paper rounds to the jar lids, and sew a granny square and button to a stack of crispy crackers. Tie on a buttoned tag telling the recipients to "Enjoy!"

CREOLE SEASONING

- 1 tablespoon salt
- 1 1/2 teaspoons garlic powder
- 1 1/2 teaspoons onion powder
- 1 1/2 teaspoons paprika
- 1 1/4 teaspoons dried thyme leaves
- 1 teaspoon ground red pepper
- 3/4 teaspoon ground black pepper
- 3/4 teaspoon dried oregano leaves
- 1/2 teaspoon crushed bay leaf
- 1/4 teaspoon chili powder

Process all ingredients in a food processor until well blended. Store in an airtight container. Use seasoning with seafood, chicken, beef, or vegetables.
Yield: about 1/4 cup

FIVE-SPICE SEASONING

- 2 teaspoons anise seeds, crushed
- 2 teaspoons ground black pepper
- 2 teaspoons fennel seeds, crushed
- 2 teaspoons ground cloves
- 2 teaspoons ground cinnamon
- 1 1/2 teaspoons ground ginger
- 1/2 teaspoon ground allspice

Combine all ingredients; store in an airtight container. Use with fish or pork.
Yield: about 1/4 cup

GROUND SEASONING

- 2 tablespoons celery seed
- 1 tablespoon onion powder
- 1 tablespoon salt

Process all ingredients in a food processor until well blended. Store in an airtight container. Use seasoning in stews, chowders, or sandwich spreads.
Yield: about 1/4 cup

GREEK SEASONING

- 2 teaspoons salt
- 2 teaspoons ground oregano
- 1 1/2 teaspoons onion powder
- 1 1/2 teaspoons garlic powder
- 1 teaspoon cornstarch
- 1 teaspoon ground black pepper
- 1 teaspoon beef bouillon granules
- 1 teaspoon dried parsley flakes
- 1/2 teaspoon ground cinnamon
- 1/2 teaspoon ground nutmeg

Process all ingredients in a food processor until well blended. Store in an airtight container. Use seasoning with steaks, pork chops, chicken, or fish.
Yield: about 1/4 cup

HERBS SEASONING

- 1 tablespoon ground thyme
- 1 tablespoon dried oregano leaves
- 2 teaspoons rubbed sage
- 1 teaspoon dried rosemary leaves
- 1 teaspoon dried marjoram leaves
- 1 teaspoon dried basil leaves
- 1 teaspoon dried parsley flakes

Process all ingredients in a food processor until well blended. Store in an airtight container. Use seasoning in omelets or on vegetables, fish, or chicken.
Yield: about 1/4 cup

"Chef's Secret"
Creole
SEASONING
from the kitchen of:
Jan Pratt

CHEF'S SECRET SEASONINGS

Mix up a bag of spices, combine with a set of flea-market-find salt & pepper shakers, a pretty towel, and a big bowl and you've got yourself a tasty housewarming gift. Just copy the label (page 156), fill in the blanks, layer with patterned cardstock, and glue to the front of white paper sack. Wrap the sack around a wooden spoon for a truly delish presentation.

APPLE-SPICE SAUCE

- 2 tablespoons butter or margarine
- 2 tablespoons firmly packed brown sugar
- $1/2$ teaspoon ground cinnamon
- 1 can (21 ounces) apple pie filling
- $1/4$ cup chopped walnuts

Combine butter, brown sugar, and cinnamon in a medium saucepan. Stirring frequently, cook over medium-low heat until butter melts. Add pie filling and increase heat to medium. Continue to stir frequently until mixture comes to a boil. Remove from heat and stir in walnuts.

Store in refrigerator. Serve warm over ice cream or cake.
Yield: about $2 1/4$ cups

PEANUT BUTTER SAUCE

- 1 cup firmly packed brown sugar
- 1 cup whipping cream
- $1/2$ cup crunchy peanut butter
- 1 teaspoon vanilla extract

Combine brown sugar and whipping cream in a medium microwave-safe bowl; whisk until smooth. Add peanut butter and microwave on HIGH 2 minutes; whisk until melted. Stir in vanilla.

Store in refrigerator. Serve warm over ice cream or cake.
Yield: about 2 cups

CHOCOLATE FUDGE SAUCE

- 2 cans (5 ounces each) evaporated milk
- 1 cup semisweet chocolate chips
- $1/2$ cup butter or margarine
- 2 cups confectioners sugar
- 1 teaspoon vanilla extract

In a large microwave-safe bowl, combine evaporated milk, chocolate chips, and butter; cover with plastic wrap. Microwave on HIGH 5 minutes; carefully remove plastic wrap and stir until smooth. Add confectioners sugar; stir until well blended. Microwave uncovered on HIGH 6 minutes, stirring every 2 minutes. Stir in vanilla.

Store in refrigerator. Serve warm over ice cream or cake.
Yield: about $2 2/3$ cups

SAUCY GIFT BAG
Purchased pound cake never tasted so good! Top a grocery store cake with these luscious sauces for a gourmet treat as a "Thank You" to a special friend. Top the lids of the 8-oz. jars with scrapbook paper and tie coordinating tags around them. Decorate a plain white gift bag with paper, cord, stickers, and jewel flowers to hold the cake and sauces.

always
there
for me

Apple-Spice
Sauce

Chocolate Fudge
Sauce

Peanut Butter
Sauce

MUSTARD PICKLES

- 1 quart whole dill pickles, drained and cut into $1/2$" slices
- 1 cup frozen chopped onions, thawed and drained
- 1 cup frozen chopped green pepper, thawed and drained
- $1/4$ cup all-purpose flour
- 1 cup water
- 1 cup white vinegar
- $1/3$ cup sugar
- 2 teaspoons dry mustard
- $1^1/2$ teaspoons salt
- 1 teaspoon ground turmeric
- 1 teaspoon celery seed
- 1 teaspoon mustard seed

In a large bowl, combine pickles, onions, and green pepper. In a medium non-aluminum saucepan, gradually whisk flour into water until mixture is smooth. Whisk in vinegar, sugar, dry mustard, salt, turmeric, celery seed, and mustard seed. Whisking frequently, bring mixture to a boil over medium-high heat. Pour hot mixture over pickles; stir until well coated. Spoon mixture into heat-resistant jars with lids; cool. Store in refrigerator.

Yield: about 5 cups

ZUCCHINI & RED PEPPER RELISH

- 1 cup canning and pickling salt
- 2 quarts cold water
- 5 medium zucchini, cut in half lengthwise and cut into $1/4$" slices
- 3 medium onions, cut into $1/4$" slices and cut in half
- 3 sweet red peppers, cut into 2" long strips
- 3 cups sugar
- 2 cups white vinegar
- 1 teaspoon celery seed
- 1 teaspoon mustard seed

In a large nonmetal bowl, stir salt into water. Place zucchini in salted water. Cover and let stand 2 hours.

Drain zucchini and thoroughly rinse with cold water. In a large bowl, combine zucchini, onions, and red pepper strips. In a large non-aluminum Dutch oven, combine sugar, vinegar, celery seed, and mustard seed. Bring vinegar mixture to a boil over high heat. Add vegetables; bring to a boil again and cook 3 minutes. Spoon mixture into heat-resistant jars with lids; cool. Store in refrigerator.

Yield: about $7^1/2$ cups

RELISH THIS!

The next time you're invited to a cookout, take jars of Mustard Pickles and Zucchini & Red Pepper Relish to the hostess. Print the labels on scrapbook paper, cut out, and glue to the rims. Cover the lids with coordinating scrapbook paper and tie with twill tape—easy peasy!

zucchini & red pepper relish

mustard pickles

PEACH FREEZER JAM

- 1 package (16 ounces) frozen peach slices, thawed
- 1 package (3 ounces) peach-flavored gelatin
- 2 tablespoons lemon juice
- $1/2$ teaspoon ascorbic powder (used to preserve fruit color)
- $4^1/2$ cups sugar
- $3/4$ cup water
- 1 package ($1^3/4$ ounces) pectin powder

In a food processor, combine peach slices, gelatin, lemon juice, and ascorbic powder; pulse process until peaches are finely chopped. In a large bowl, combine sugar and fruit mixture; let stand 10 minutes.

In a 1-quart microwave-safe bowl or measuring cup, combine water and pectin; microwave on HIGH 2 to $2^1/2$ minutes or until mixture boils. Microwave another 45 seconds; stir. Microwave 15 seconds longer; stir. Pour hot pectin mixture into fruit mixture; stir 3 minutes. Pour into clean jars to within $1/2$" of tops; wipe off rims of jars. Screw on lids. Allow jam to stand at room temperature for 24 hours; store in freezer.

Place in refrigerator 1 hour before serving. May be refrozen. Keeps up to 3 weeks in refrigerator or up to 1 year in freezer.

Yield: about $6^1/2$ cups

FOR A PEACH OF A FRIEND

Recycled and vintage jars look "peachy keen" when filled with easy-to-make Peach Freezer Jam. Decorate the jars with peach-colored rickrack and ribbon. Farm-fresh scrapbook paper and cardstock tags (tied on with embroidery floss) complete the sunny look.

Disappearing Snacks

FIESTA SNACK MIX

- 1 bag (9.25 ounces) corn chips
- 1 can (11.5 ounces) mixed salted nuts
- ¼ cup butter or margarine, melted
- ¼ cup grated Parmesan cheese
- 2 teaspoons taco seasoning mix

In a large bowl, combine corn chips and nuts. In a small bowl, combine butter, cheese, and taco seasoning mix; pour over corn chip mixture. Stir until well coated. Spread mixture evenly on a baking pan.

Bake at 325° for 12 minutes. Cool completely.

Yield: about 7 cups

ZESTY SNACK MIX

- 2 packages (6.6 ounces each) fish-shaped Cheddar cheese crackers
- 1 package (8 ounces) fish-shaped pretzels
- 2 cups slivered almonds
- ¾ cup butter or margarine, melted
- 1 package (1 ounce) ranch-style salad dressing mix
- 1 package (1.25 ounces) garlic Alfredo sauce mix

Combine crackers, pretzels, and almonds in a medium roasting pan. In a small bowl, combine melted butter and dry mixes; pour over dry ingredients. Stir until well coated.

Bake at 300° for 30 minutes, stirring every 10 minutes. Allow to cool.

Yield: about 12 cups

SNACK MIX BAGS

Festive cellophane bags of snack mix are fun at any summertime party. Layer colorful punched cardstock ovals, stamp a message or greeting, and attach to the bagged mix. Bright pails, lined with cheerful towels, are fun take-home reminders of the party.

FRESH SALSA VERDE

1 pound fresh tomatillos, hulled and finely chopped
3/4 cup finely chopped onion
1/4 cup water
1/2 teaspoon salt
1 avocado, seeded, peeled, and chopped
1/4 cup chopped fresh cilantro
2 tablespoons freshly squeezed lime juice
2 to 3 garlic cloves, minced
1 small fresh jalapeño pepper, seeded and chopped
1/4 teaspoon black pepper
Tortilla chips to serve

In a medium saucepan over medium heat, combine tomatillos, onion, water, and salt. Cover and cook about 15 minutes or until tomatillos are tender; drain. In a medium bowl, combine tomatillo mixture, avocado, cilantro, lime juice, garlic, jalapeño pepper, and black pepper. Cover and chill 2 hours to allow flavors to blend.

Serve salsa with tortilla chips.

Yield: about 2 cups

CHERRY SALSA

This salsa would also make a good accompaniment to grilled meat.

2 cans (15 ounces each) dark, sweet, pitted cherries in heavy syrup, drained and coarsely chopped
3 tablespoons chopped red onion
3 tablespoons chopped fresh basil leaves
3 tablespoons finely chopped green pepper
3 tablespoons honey
2 tablespoons finely chopped fresh jalapeño pepper
1 tablespoon freshly squeezed lime juice
1 teaspoon grated lime zest
1/2 teaspoon salt
Tortilla chips to serve

In a medium bowl, combine cherries, onion, basil, green pepper, honey, jalapeño pepper, lime juice, lime zest, and salt. Cover and chill 2 hours to allow flavors to blend.

Serve salsa with tortilla chips.

Yield: about 2 cups

SOUTH OF THE BORDER GIFT BASKET

Jar up one of these salsas and add a sassy label to the lid with scrapbook paper, chipboard letters, and a button-centered flower. Add fresh limes, a drink mix, bagged chips, and a vibrant towel—let the party begin!

GARDEN FRESH TOTE

A burlap tote brimming with fresh veggies and dip gets even more dressed up with a cardstock tag that's been decorated with a chipboard flower, highlighted around the edges with colored pencil, and tied on with rickrack.

ROASTED OLIVE DIP

- ½ cup whole stuffed green olives, drained
- ½ cup Kalamata olives, drained and pitted
- 5 tablespoons Greek vinaigrette salad dressing, divided
- 1 package (8 ounces) cream cheese, softened
- ½ cup sour cream
- ½ cup mayonnaise
- ½ teaspoon Greek seasoning
  Toasted pita wedges to serve

Combine olives and 4 tablespoons salad dressing in an 8" square baking pan. Stirring every 10 minutes, bake olives at 400° for about 25 minutes or until lightly browned and wrinkled; cool.

Drain and coarsely chop olives. In a medium bowl, beat cream cheese, sour cream, and mayonnaise until well blended. Add remaining 1 tablespoon salad dressing and Greek seasoning. Stir in chopped olives. Chill 2 hours to allow flavors to blend.

Serve olive dip at room temperature with pita wedges.

Yield: about 2½ cups

ONION-BACON DIP

- 2 cups sour cream
- 2 cups mayonnaise
- 1 envelope (1 ounce) dry onion soup mix
- 1½ teaspoons garlic powder
- 1 jar (2.8 ounces) real bacon pieces (reserve 1 tablespoon for garnish, if desired)
  Garnishes: fresh parsley, bacon pieces
  Fresh vegetables to serve

In a medium bowl, combine sour cream, mayonnaise, soup mix, and garlic powder; stir until well blended. Reserving 1 tablespoon bacon if garnishing, stir in remaining bacon. Cover and refrigerate 8 hours or overnight to allow flavors to blend.

Garnish, if desired. Serve with fresh vegetables.

Yield: about 4 cups

SWEET & SAVORY NUTS

Reward the leaf rakers with a vintage milk bottle of spicy (or sweet) nuts. Just fill the bottle with the pecans, add a scrapbook paper cap (tied on with red and natural jute twine) and personalize it with a felt-backed (circle pattern, page 150) monogram brad. A label with rub-on letters, attached to a rusty mini pail, is a great final touch.

Peppery Pecans

GOURMET HONEY-ROASTED NUTS

- 3/4 cup honey
- 1/4 cup sugar
- 3 tablespoons butter or margarine
- 1/4 teaspoon dried orange peel
- 1 teaspoon vanilla extract
- 1 cup whole unsalted macadamia nuts
- 1 cup whole unsalted hazelnuts
- 1 cup whole unsalted cashews
- 1 cup unsalted pecan halves
- Sugar

In a large saucepan, combine honey, 1/4 cup sugar, butter, orange peel, and vanilla. Stirring constantly, cook over medium heat until sugar dissolves. Stir in nuts. Spread nuts on a greased jellyroll pan.

Stirring once, bake at 350° for 25 to 30 minutes or until golden brown. Cool completely on pan. Break into pieces. Roll in additional sugar.
Yield: about 6 cups

PEPPERY PECANS

- 4 cups pecan halves
- 1/3 cup butter or margarine, melted
- 1 tablespoon Worcestershire sauce
- 1 teaspoon salt
- 3/4 teaspoon ground red pepper
- 3/4 teaspoon ground black pepper

Place pecans on an ungreased jellyroll pan. In a small bowl, combine melted butter, Worcestershire sauce, salt, red pepper, and black pepper. Pour mixture over pecans, stirring to coat. Spread pecans in a single layer.

Bake at 300° for 15 minutes, stirring every 5 minutes. Cool on pan.
Yield: about 4 cups

REUBEN SPREAD

- 1 package (8 ounces) cream cheese, softened
- 1/4 cup seafood cocktail sauce
- 1 cup (4 ouces) shredded Swiss cheese
- 1/4 pound deli corned beef, finely chopped
- 3/4 cup sauerkraut, drained and chopped

In a medium bowl, beat cream cheese and cocktail sauce until smooth. Stir in remaining ingredients, blending thoroughly. Store in refrigerator. Serve with cocktail rye bread slices or rye crackers.

Yield: about 2 1/2 cups

SESAME SPREAD WITH TOASTED PITA CHIPS

Coconut, chutney, almonds, or golden raisins are excellent toppings for this tasty spread!

- 1 can (15 ounces) garbanzo beans, drained
- 1/3 cup tahini (sesame seed paste)
- 1/3 cup lemon juice
- 1/4 cup chopped green onion
- 1 tablespoon minced fresh parsley
- 1 garlic clove, minced
- 1/4 teaspoon salt
- 1/4 teaspoon ground black pepper
  Pita bread

Combine beans, tahini, lemon juice, green onion, parsley, garlic, salt, and pepper in a blender or food processor and process until smooth. Spoon mixture into a small bowl; cover and refrigerate at least 1 hour.

Slice pita rounds in half horizontally. Cut each circle into 8 wedges. Place on ungreased baking sheet. Bake at 450° for 5 to 8 minutes or until lightly browned and crisp. Serve sesame spread with pita chips.

Yield: about 1 1/2 cups

HEARTY SPREADS

Show Dad how much you appreciate him with a hearty, game time snack. Line a lunchbox-style mesh container with fall-themed scrapbook paper. Spoon the spreads into small jars and decorate the lids with layered scrapbook paper circles. Place bagged chips, crackers, and other favorite snacks in the container along with the spreads. Tie a few ribbons and trims around the container handle and Dad's ready for the big game.

CARAWAY WAFERS

    1   cup all-purpose flour
    1   teaspoon dry mustard
  1/4   teaspoon salt
  1/2   cup shredded Swiss cheese
    2   teaspoons caraway seed
  1/2   teaspoon paprika
  1/4   teaspoon cayenne pepper
  1/3   cup butter or margarine, softened
    3   tablespoons cold water
    1   teaspoon Worcestershire sauce
        Paprika

In a medium bowl, combine flour, dry mustard, and salt. Stir in cheese, caraway seed, 1/2 teaspoon paprika, and cayenne. Cut in butter until mixture resembles coarse meal. Add water and Worcestershire sauce; blend with a fork until dough sticks together, adding more water if necessary. Shape into a ball.

On a lightly floured surface, roll out dough to 1/8" thickness. Use a 1 1/2" biscuit cutter to cut out dough. Place on an ungreased baking sheet. Sprinkle tops with paprika. Bake in a preheated 425° oven for 5 to 7 minutes or until lightly browned. Cool on a wire rack.

Yield: about 4 dozen

SMOKY CHEESE BITES

    2   cups all-purpose flour
  1/2   teaspoon salt
  1/4   teaspoon cayenne pepper
    8   ounces smoked Cheddar cheese,
        shredded
    1   cup butter or margarine, softened
    1   can (6 ounces) hickory-flavored
        whole almonds

In a large bowl, combine flour, salt, and pepper. Add cheese, mixing well. Cut in butter until mixture resembles a coarse meal. Knead dough with hands until smooth.

On a lightly floured surface, roll out dough to 1/4" thickness. Use a 1 1/2" biscuit cutter to cut out dough. Place on greased baking sheets, topping each with an almond. Bake in a preheated 375° oven for 8 to 10 minutes or until bottoms are lightly browned. Cool on wire racks.

Yield: about 5 dozen

HAPPY HOUR TIDBITS

For a cozy night in, give these nutty cheese crackers with a block of aged cheese, spicy sausage, and a fine wine, all nestled in a rustic basket along with a small cutting board. Place the crackers in a cellophane bag and top with a folded cardstock label that's embellished with diamond-shaped brads and rub-on letters.

NUTTY BLUE CHEESE SPREAD

   1   package (8 ounces) cream cheese,
         softened
   1   package (4 ounces) blue cheese,
         crumbled
   2   tablespoons sour cream
   1/4 teaspoon ground red pepper
   1/4 cup finely chopped celery
   1/4 cup finely chopped green onion
   1   cup chopped walnuts, toasted and
         finely chopped

Process cream cheese, blue cheese, sour cream, and red pepper in a food processor until smooth. Add celery, green onions, and walnuts; process just until blended. Cover and refrigerate 2 hours to allow flavors to blend.

Store in refrigerator. Serve at room temperature with crackers.

Yield: about 2¹/₄ cups

BOURSIN CHEESE SPREAD

   2   packages (8 ounces each) cream cheese,
         softened
   1   cup butter, softened
   2   garlic cloves, minced
   1   teaspoon dried oregano leaves
   1   teaspoon dried basil leaves
   1/4 teaspoon dried dill weed
   1/4 teaspoon dried marjoram leaves
   1/4 teaspoon dried thyme leaves
   1/4 teaspoon ground black pepper

Combine all ingredients, blending until smooth. Cover and refrigerate overnight to allow flavors to blend.

Store in refrigerator. Serve at room temperature with crackers.

Yield: about 3 cups

SPREAD SOME HAPPINESS

Celebrate a neighbor's retirement and travel plans with a jar of flavorful cheese spread. Place the cheese in an old-school canning jar decked out with ribbons, a layered cardstock tag, and a vintage spreader.

CINNAMON SNACK MIX

    3 cups apple-cinnamon-flavored cereal
    2 cups pecan halves
    1 cup whole almonds
    1 cup chow mein noodles
    2 egg whites
    1 cup sugar
    2 tablespoons ground cinnamon
  $1/2$ teaspoon salt

In a large bowl, combine cereal, pecans, almonds, and noodles. In a small bowl, combine egg whites, sugar, cinnamon, and salt; pour over dry ingredients. Stir until well coated. Spread on a greased baking sheet. Bake at 225° for 35 to 40 minutes, stirring frequently. Spread on waxed paper to cool.
Yield: about 9 cups

CHEESY SNACK MIX

   14 cups (about 20 ounces) small
       pretzels
    1 cup butter or margarine
    1 cup grated Parmesan cheese
    3 packages (1.25 ounces each) cheese
       sauce mix
    2 packages (1 ounce each) ranch-style
       salad dressing mix
    1 teaspoon garlic powder

Place pretzels in a large bowl. In a saucepan, melt butter; remove from heat and stir in remaining ingredients. Pour over pretzels; stir until well coated. Spread mixture on 2 ungreased baking sheets. Bake at 350° for 10 to 12 minutes or until golden brown.
Yield: about $15^1/2$ cups

SNACK ON
Any glass container can be dressed up with cardstock stickers. Fill the canister with a flavorful snack mix and add a cute tag labeled with the snack mix name before delivery.

cinnamon snack mix

Pecan Butter Spread

PECAN BUTTER SPREAD

- 1¹/₄ cups chopped pecans
- 2 tablespoons peanut oil
- 8 ounces Brie cheese, rind removed
- 1 package (3 ounces) cream cheese, softened
- 2 tablespoons sherry
- ¹/₄ teaspoon salt
  Crackers, apples, and Roasted Pecans to serve

Process pecans and peanut oil in a food processor until smooth. Add Brie cheese, cream cheese, sherry, and salt; process until mixture is completely blended.

Serve at room temperature with crackers and apple slices; top with Roasted Pecans. Store in refrigerator.
Yield: about 1¹/₂ cups

ROASTED PECANS

- 1 cup pecan halves
- 1 tablespoon butter, melted
  Salt

In a small bowl, combine pecans and butter. Spread nuts on an ungreased baking sheet and bake at 200° for 1 hour, stirring every 15 minutes. Drain on paper towel; sprinkle with salt.
Yield: 1 cup

SPREAD SOME LOVE

What do you get when you mix cheese, crackers, apples, pecans, and a whole lotta love? A great "I thought of you today" gift! Just bag up some crackers and roasted pecans (top the bags with dotty cardstock and ribbon- & button-trimmed clothespins) and place them in a pottery bowl along with a small pail of tasty pecan butter spread. Use the same dotty cardstock, rub-on letters, and ribbon to make a label to tie the cellophane bag closed.

MOVIE NIGHT

What's Movie Night without popcorn—especially gourmet popcorn! Either paint or wrap a shoebox with colored paper and add a band of upholstery webbing. Attach a loopy badge made with twill tape, a chipboard "4", and a hand-lettered "Movie Night" tag. Bag up the flavored popcorn and place in popcorn boxes (found in the party section of the craft store). A movie (or two) and some candy complete the gift.

RUM POPCORN

9	cups popped popcorn
1	cup mixed nuts
1/2	cup butter or margarine
1	cup firmly packed brown sugar
1/2	cup light corn syrup
1 1/2	teaspoons rum extract
1	teaspoon baking soda

Combine popcorn and nuts in a lightly greased large, shallow baking pan. In a medium saucepan, bring butter, sugar, and corn syrup to a boil over medium-high heat; cook 5 minutes. Remove from heat; stir in extract and baking soda. Pour mixture over popcorn and nuts; stir well. Bake at 250° for 1 hour, stirring every 15 minutes. Spread on waxed paper. Cool completely and break into bite-size pieces.

Yield: about 10 cups

ALMOND CARAMEL CORN

2	cups whole unsalted almonds
	Vegetable cooking spray
16	cups popped popcorn
1	cup firmly packed brown sugar
2	tablespoons light corn syrup
2	tablespoons molasses
1	teaspoon almond extract
1/2	teaspoon salt
1/2	teaspoon baking soda

To toast almonds, place almonds on an ungreased baking sheet. Stirring occasionally, bake at 350° for 8 to 10 minutes or until almonds are slightly darker in color. Cool completely on baking sheet.

Spray inside of a 14" x 20" oven cooking bag with cooking spray. Place popcorn and almonds in bag. In a 2-quart microwave-safe bowl, combine next 3 ingredients. Microwave on HIGH 2 minutes or until mixture boils. Stir and microwave 2 minutes longer. Stir in remaining ingredients. Pour syrup over popcorn mixture; stir and shake until well coated. Microwave 1 1/2 minutes. Stir, shake, and microwave 1 1/2 minutes longer. Spread on aluminum foil sprayed with cooking spray. Cool completely and break into bite-size pieces.

Yield: about 18 cups

YOGURT CHEESE SPREAD

1	container (32 ounces) plain low-fat yogurt
1/4	cup minced green onion
3	tablespoons reduced-calorie mayonnaise
1	tablespoon chopped fresh parsley
1	garlic clove, minced
1	teaspoon Worcestershire sauce
1/4	teaspoon salt
1/8	teaspoon ground black pepper
1/8	teaspoon cayenne pepper

To make yogurt cheese, place a colander over a large glass or ceramic bowl. Line colander with 4 layers of cheesecloth; spoon yogurt into colander. Cover with plastic wrap and refrigerate 12 hours to allow liquid to drain.

Spoon yogurt cheese into a container, discarding liquid.

To make Yogurt Cheese Spread, combine 1 cup yogurt cheese with remaining ingredients in a small bowl. Stir well to blend (do not beat or use a food processor). Cover and refrigerate 8 hours or overnight to allow flavors to blend.

Serve with Guilt-Free Snack Chips or fresh vegetables. Store in refrigerator.

Yield: about 1¹/₂ cups

GUILT-FREE SNACK CHIPS

1	package (10 ounces) flour tortillas
	Vegetable oil cooking spray
1/4	cup low-calorie Italian salad dressing
	Garlic salt or salt-free herb and spice blend

Cut each tortilla into eighths. Place on a baking sheet lightly sprayed with cooking spray. Use a pastry brush to spread salad dressing over tops of pieces. Sprinkle with garlic salt or herb blend. Bake at 325° for 10 to 12 minutes or until lightly browned.

Yield: about 7 cups

GOOD FOR YOU SNACKS

Encourage a friend's healthy eating goals with a dish towel-lined container filled with colorful plates, a jar of herbed Yogurt Cheese Spread, some homemade Snack Chips, and freshly cut veggie sticks. Place the plastic-bagged dippers in a white gift bag. Decorate a wooden clothespin and use it to clip a folded cardstock topper (trimmed with rickrack) to the gift bag.

Guilt-Free
Snack Chips

Yogurt Cheese
Spread

general instructions

Sizing Patterns

All the patterns in this book are the size we used on our projects. You can make the patterns larger or smaller to suit your needs. Here's how:

1. To change the size of the pattern, divide the desired height of the pattern by the actual height of the pattern. Multiply the result by 100 and photocopy the pattern at this percentage.

For example: You want your pattern to be 8"h, but the pattern on the page is 6"h.

  8÷6=1.33
  1.33 x 100=133%.
  Copy the pattern at 133%.

2. If your copier doesn't enlarge to the size you need, enlarge the pattern to the maximum percentage on the copier. Then repeat step 1, dividing the desired size by the size of the enlarged pattern. Multiply this result by 100 and photocopy the enlarged pattern at the new percentage. Repeat as needed to reach the desired size and tape the pattern pieces together.

Making Patterns

Place tracing paper or tissue paper over the pattern and draw over the lines. For a more durable pattern, use a permanent marker to draw over the pattern on stencil plastic.

Transferring Patterns To Fabrics

Trace the pattern onto tissue paper. Pin the tissue paper to the fabric and stitch through the paper. Carefully tear the tissue paper away.

Transferring Patterns To Cardstock Or Other Materials

Trace the pattern onto tracing paper; cut out. Place the pattern on the cardstock (or whatever material you are transferring to) and use a pencil to lightly draw around the pattern. For pattern details, slip transfer paper between the pattern and the cardstock and draw over the detail lines.

Making Fusible Appliqués

Leaving at least 1/2" between shapes, trace the patterns onto the paper side of fusible web. Cut shapes apart about 1/4" outside the traced lines and fuse each shape to the wrong side of the fabrics. Cut out the shapes along the drawn lines and remove the paper backing.

Embroidery Stitches

Follow the stitch diagrams to bring the needle up at 1 and all odd numbers and down at 2 and all even numbers, unless otherwise indicated.

Backstitch

Bring the needle up at 1, go down at 2, and come up at 3 (*Fig. 1*).

Fig. 1

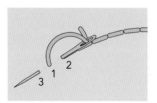

Blanket Stitch

Referring to **Fig. 2**, bring the needle up at 1. Keeping the thread below the point of the needle, go down at 2, and come up at 3. Continue working as shown in **Fig. 3**.

Fig. 2

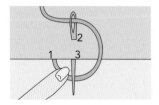

Fig. 3

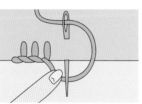

Chain Stitch

Referring to **Fig. 4**, bring the needle up at 1, go down again at 1, forming a loop and keeping the thread below the point of the needle. Come up at 2, and go down again at 2 to form a second loop. Continue working as shown; anchor the last loop with a small straight stitch.

Fig. 4

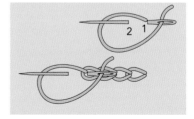

Cross Stitch

Referring to **Fig. 5**, bring the needle up at 1, go down at 2, come up at 3, and go down at 4.

Fig. 5

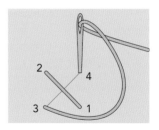

French Knot

Referring to **Fig. 6**, bring the needle up at 1. Wrap the floss once around the needle and insert the needle at 2, holding the floss end with non-stitching fingers. Tighten the knot; then, pull the needle through the fabric, holding the floss until it must be released. For a larger knot, use more strands; wrap only once.

Fig. 6

Running Stitch

Referring to **Fig. 7**, make a series of straight stitches with the stitch length equal to the space between stitches.

Fig. 7

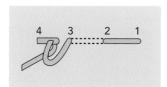

Satin Stitch

Bring the needle up at 1, go down at 2, come up at 3, and go down at 4 (*Fig. 8*).

Fig. 8

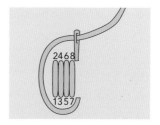

Stem Stitch

Referring to **Fig. 9**, come up at 1. Keeping the thread below the stitching line, go down at 2 and come up at 3.

Fig. 9

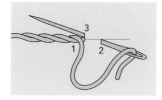

Straight Stitch

Referring to **Fig. 10**, come up at 1 and go down at 2.

Fig. 10

Coiled Rag Coaster

(also shown on page 89)

For each 4" coaster, you'll need:
- 2 yds $^3/_{16}$" dia. poly-reinforced cotton clothesline
- $^1/_8$ yard fabric
- contrasting color sewing thread
- rotary cutter, rotary ruler, and cutting mat
- size 90/14 sharp sewing machine needle

1. Use the rotary cutter, ruler, and mat to cut fabric into $^1/_2$" wide strips, cutting selvage to selvage.

2. Wrap one clothesline cord end with a fabric strip and zigzag stitch, catching the cord in the stitching *(Fig. 1)*.

3. Wrap the fabric strip around the cord, angling the fabric as you wrap toward your body. When you get to the end of the fabric strip, pin the loose end in place.

4. Fold about $^1/_2$" of the cord to the left and place the fold under the presser foot. Using a wide stitch width and short stitch length, zigzag stitch the folded area *(Fig. 2)*.

Fig. 2

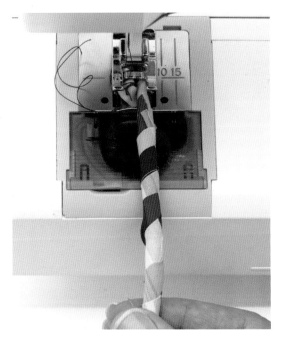

Fig. 1

5. Continue zigzag stitching the cord together, pivoting the work as you sew *(Fig. 3)*.

Fig. 3

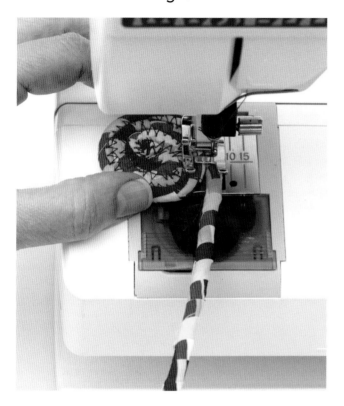

6. To add a new fabric strip, ovelap the old strip by about ¹/₂" *(Fig. 4)* and continue wrapping, zigzag stitching, and pivoting until the coaster is about 4" in diameter.

Fig. 4

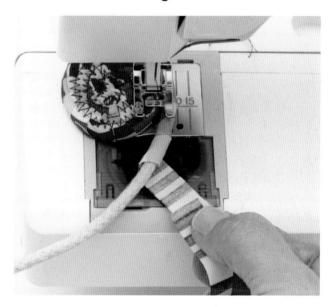

7. Cut the cord and fabric strip, leaving a 4" length of fabric. Wrap the cord end with the fabric, zigzag stitch over the cord end, and trim the excess fabric.

Ribbon Rose

(also shown on page 39)

For each ribbon rose you'll need:
- a felt scrap
- 1/2 yard of 1 1/2" wide wire-edged ribbon
- hot glue gun
- pin back

1. Cut a 1 3/4" diameter felt circle for the base.
2. Twist and hot glue one ribbon end to the base circle center (*Fig. 1*).

Fig. 1

3. Working in a spiraling motion, twist and glue the ribbon to the base circle (*Figs. 2-3*). Continue until the felt is covered; trim any excess ribbon and glue the end down.

Fig. 2

Fig. 3

4. Hot glue the pin back to the rose wrong side.

patterns

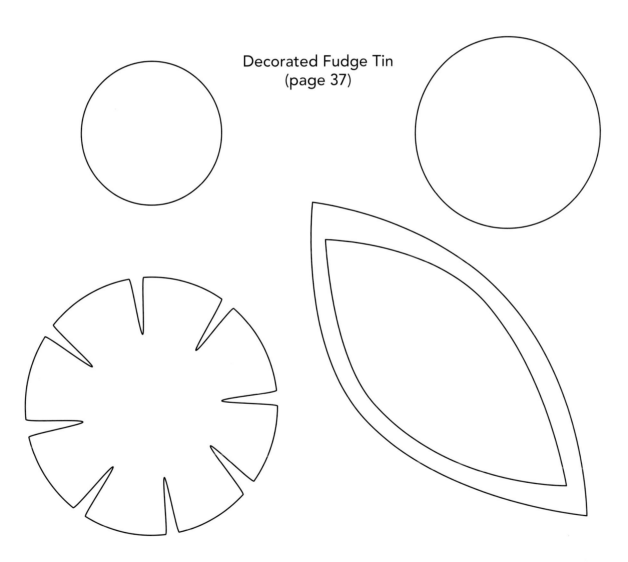

Decorated Fudge Tin
(page 37)

Sweet & Savory Nuts
(page 126)

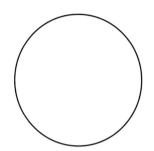

Bottle Bag
(page 7)

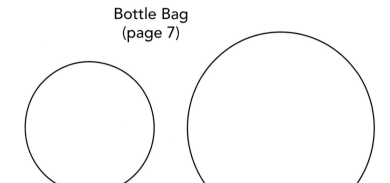

Cheery Thanks
(page 59)

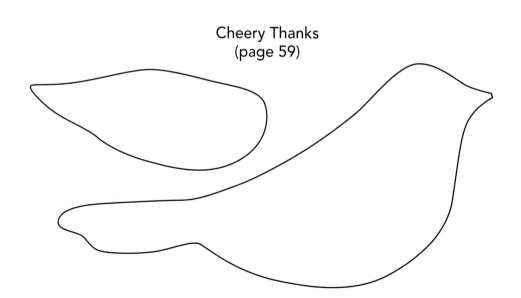

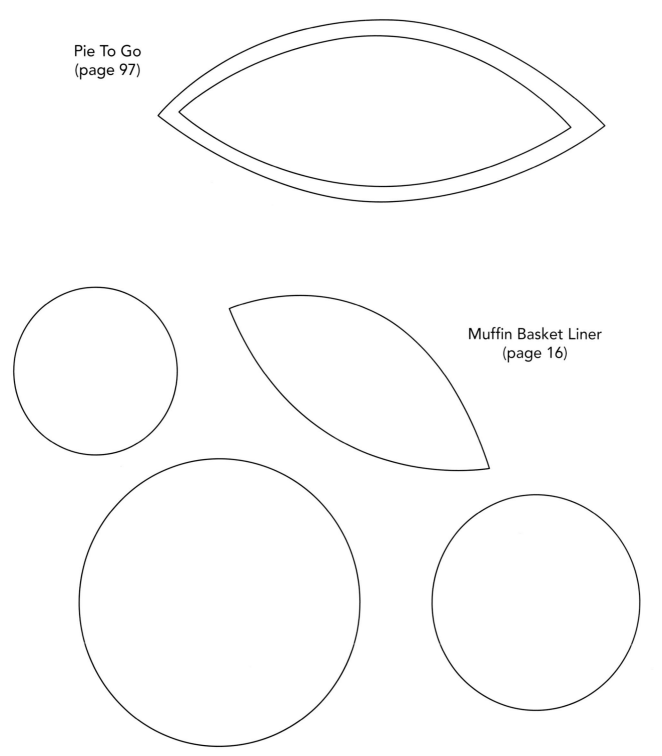

Pie To Go
(page 97)

Muffin Basket Liner
(page 16)

Appliquéd Tea Towel
(page 21)

╱ Satin Stitch	╱ Chain Stitch
╱ Blanket Stitch	╱ Straight Stitch
● French Knot	╱ Stem Stitch
	⊙ Buttons

Homemade Goodness
(page 107)

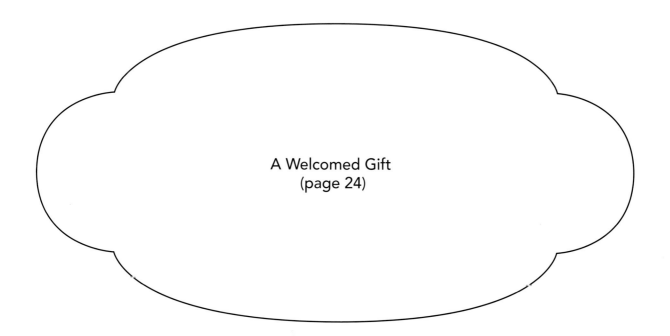

A Welcomed Gift
(page 24)

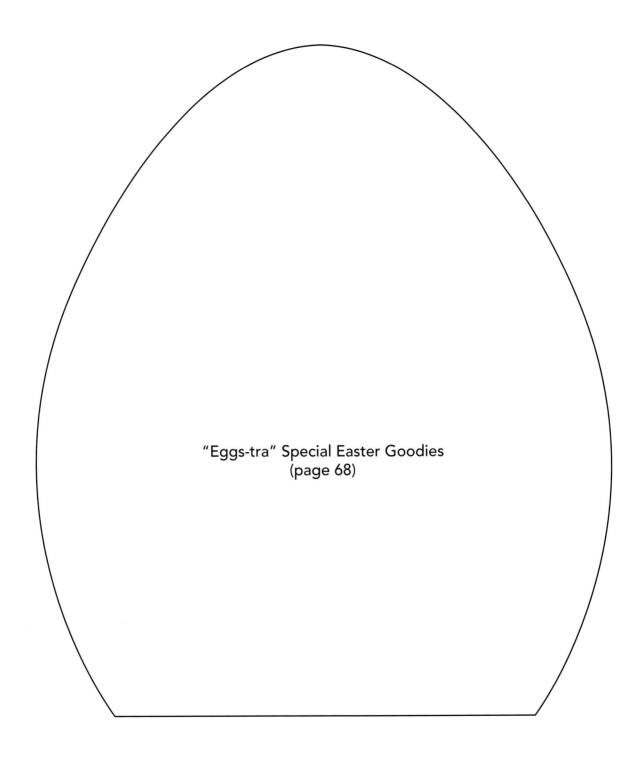

"Eggs-tra" Special Easter Goodies
(page 68)

Summertime Treats
(page 53)

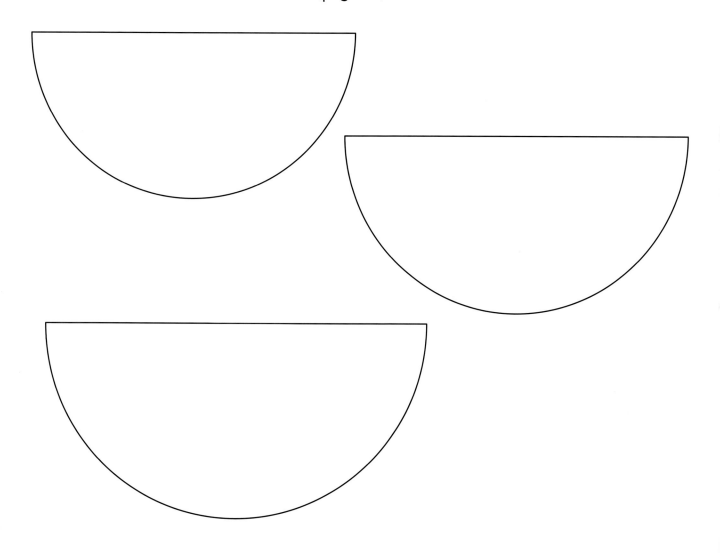

"Chef's Secret"

SEASONING

from the kitchen of:

Chef's Secret Seasonings
(page 113)

Cookie Cones
(page 76)

Be My Valentine
(page 63)

Playing with the Queen
of Hearts
(page 64)

COOKING TIPS

Measuring Ingredients

Liquid measuring cups have a rim above the measuring line to keep liquid ingredients from spilling. Nested measuring cups are used to measure dry ingredients, butter, shortening, and peanut butter. Measuring spoons are used for measuring both dry and liquid ingredients.

- *To measure flour or granulated sugar:* Spoon ingredient into nested measuring cup and level off with a knife. Do not pack down with spoon.
- *To measure confectioners sugar:* Sift sugar, spoon lightly into nested measuring cup, and level off with a knife.
- *To measure brown sugar:* Pack sugar into nested measuring cup and level off with a knife. Sugar should hold its shape when removed from cup.
- *To measure butter, shortening, or peanut butter:* Pack ingredient firmly into nested measuring cup and level off with a knife.
- *To measure liquids:* Use a liquid measuring cup placed on a flat surface. Pour ingredient into cup and check measuring line at eye level.
- *To measure honey or syrup:* For a more accurate measurement, lightly spray measuring cup or spoon with cooking spray before measuring so the liquid will release easily from cup or spoon.

Tests For Candy Making

To determine the correct temperature of cooked candy, use a candy thermometer and the cold water test. Before each use, check the accuracy of your candy thermometer by attaching it to the side of a small saucepan of water, making sure thermometer does not touch bottom of pan. Bring water to a boil. Thermometer should register 212° when water begins to boil. If it does not, adjust the temperature range for each candy consistency accordingly.

When using a candy thermometer, insert thermometer into candy mixture, making sure thermometer does not touch bottom of pan. Read temperature at eye level. Cook candy to desired temperature range. Working quickly, drop about $1/2$ teaspoon of candy mixture into a cup of ice water. Use a fresh cup of water for each test. Use the following descriptions to determine if candy has reached the correct consistency:

- *Soft-Ball Stage (234°-240°):* Candy will easily form a ball in ice water but will flatten when held in your hand.
- *Firm-Ball Stage (242°-248°):* Candy will form a firm ball in ice water but will flatten if pressed when removed from the water.
- *Hard-Ball Stage (250°-268°):* Candy will form a hard ball in ice water and will remain hard when removed from the water.
- *Soft-Crack Stage (270°-290°):* Candy will form hard threads in ice water but will soften when removed from the water.
- *Hard-Crack Stage (300°-310°):* Candy will form brittle threads in ice water and will remain brittle when removed from the water.

Preparing Citrus Fruit Zest

To remove outer portion of peel (colored part) from citrus fruits, use a fine grater or fruit zester, being careful not to cut into the bitter white portion. Zest is also referred to as grated peel.

Toasting Nuts

To toast nuts, spread nuts on an ungreased baking sheet. Stirring occasionally, bake 8 to 10 minutes in a preheated 350° oven until nuts are slightly darker in color.

recipe index

Continued on page 160